Contents

P...
AF...
TO...
in ... ol

Mary A. Bean & Paul Wagstaff

LONGMAN

The Authors

Mary A. Bean has spent much of her teaching career focusing on children's language development. She has undertaken much research in the field of children's writing and has led Authority INSET courses on a variety of curricular issues. She lectures part-time at Bradford and Ilkley Community College. She achieved an M.Ed degree at Leeds University in 1985 and is now headteacher at Parkwood First School in Keighley.

Paul Wagstaff has a long-established interest in the field of multicultural education. His involvement in the Bradford Education for All Working Party and his research and lecturing on the subject at Leeds University has complemented his experience as a practising teacher. He has run INSET courses on a variety of curricular issues. He achieved an M.Ed degree at Leeds University in 1987 and is now headteacher at Whitecote Primary School in Leeds.

ISBN 0 582 066 328 ✓

First published 1991

©Longman Group UK Ltd

Set in Palacio and Triumvirate
Typeset by Typewise Photosetting, York
Printed in Great Britain by Longman York Publishing Services

Acknowledgements

This book owes a great deal to our many close friends and teacher colleagues who together have explored our ideas and feelings and have shared in our vision of writing development. Many of the practical examples and case studies owe much to their work. Without their support in developing our ideas and projects, many of the illustrated case studies would not have been possible. Particular thanks are extended to Maggie Power and Cath Robinson for their support and practical help with the case study 'The Bilingual Storyteller' and to the author Gerald Rose for permission to use his work as the basis of our case study 'The Unfriendly Game'.

The book makes wide use of the work of the children from Wellington, Reevy Hill and Grange Road First Schools in Bradford and Kirkburton Middle School in Kirklees. We are indebted to them for this and would like to thank them for all the enjoyment they have provided as we have shared their journeys into literacy.

A particular thank you is expressed to the following individuals who, over time, have encouraged and inspired many of the ideas expressed in this book: Douglas Barnes, Roger Beard, Archie Barrett, Jean Blackburn, Jenny Leach, Melissa Passey and Geoff Rowe.

Many of our case studies have involved a number of outside agencies in the pursuit of the first-hand experience and we would like to acknowledge colleagues from these with whom we have shared many of our experiences. They are:

Bradford Countryside Warden Service
Bradford Museum of Film, Photography and Television
Bradford Media Working Party
Bradford Education for All Working Party
Ingleborough Hall Outdoor Education Centre
Clarke Hall, Wakefield
Dorset Street Centre, Bradford

Our heartfelt thanks go to Judith Martin for her patience in typing our manuscript.

More than anyone else, we are indebted to both our families, particularly Jill and Doug, who have supported us throughout the writing of this book and we would like to acknowledge how difficult our work would have been without that support.

Acknowledgements

This book owes a great deal to our many close friends and teacher colleagues who together have explored our ideas and feelings and have shared in our vision of writing development. Many of the practical examples and case studies owe much to their work. Without their support in developing our ideas and projects, many of the illustrated case studies would not have been possible. Particular thanks are extended to Maggie Power and Cath Robinson for their support and practical help with the case study 'The Bilingual Storyteller' and to the author Gerald Rose for permission to use his work as the basis of our case study 'The Unfriendly Game'.

The book makes wide use of the work of the children from Wellington, Reevy Hill and Grange Road First Schools in Bradford and Kirkburton Middle School in Kirklees. We are indebted to them for this and would like to thank them for all the enjoyment they have provided as we have shared their journeys into literacy.

A particular thank you is expressed to the following individuals who, over time, have encouraged and inspired many of the ideas expressed in this book: Douglas Barnes, Roger Beard, Archie Barrett, Jean Blackburn, Jenny Leach, Melissa Passey and Geoff Rowe.

Many of our case studies have involved a number of outside agencies in the pursuit of the first-hand experience and we would like to acknowledge colleagues from these with whom we have shared many of our experiences. They are:

Bradford Countryside Warden Service
Bradford Museum of Film, Photography and Television
Bradford Media Working Party
Bradford Education for All Working Party
Ingleborough Hall Outdoor Education Centre
Clarke Hall, Wakefield
Dorset Street Centre, Bradford

Our heartfelt thanks go to Judith Martin for her patience in typing our manuscript.

More than anyone else, we are indebted to both our families, particularly Jill and Doug, who have supported us throughout the writing of this book and we would like to acknowledge how difficult our work would have been without that support.

Introduction

One of the chief pleasures we have found in teaching has been that of reading the literature children produce. We have often felt privileged to be involved with them in their writing and to share their ephemeral products. One of the cruellest aspects of learning to write however is that the product, like the mayfly, is short-lived. Much of the written creativity produced by children is often not appreciated by a wider audience; so often stories and poems which reflect highly original ideas and creative use of language are lost from school at the end of the year as display boards are cleared and children take their work home. Therefore, no matter how delightful the end-product is, however, the main concern for teachers must surely be with the *process* of writing and an understanding of the development of that process. Only by understanding the development of this process can teachers encourage children in the development and production of depth and quality in their writing. As we observe children writing, we often feel that a window has opened on to their minds but we never gain a complete picture of how the child's thoughts occur in the first place and how they are transferred from head to paper. Research in the past has been mainly concerned with the interrelationship between the cognitive and affective aspects of development and how they are revealed in writing. We argue throughout this book that if children are introduced to different kinds of writing and a breadth of writing experience, they are encouraged to explore rational and emotional ideas to different extents and to attend to the many cognitive demands that present themselves in the variety of situations they will experience daily. The writing they produce will display evidence of quality, tempered by many differing feelings and emotions.

In the classroom situation some teachers are now encouraging children to write for a variety of different purposes, but we are aware of the lack of research in certain areas. Only recently has there been any guidance for the practising teacher in developing persuasive writing with children (for example research in Canada by the York/OISE group led by Bereiter and Scardamalia in 1985).

There is widespread recognition of the lack of real balance between writing demands and purposes in schools and the area of persuasive writing in particular is undervalued in the primary years. Frank Smith (1984c) feels that as teachers we should develop critical thinking, so much a part of persuasive writing, in school, as he observed that his own students were unable to express critical thoughts in writing. When he asked them for a written argument, they had little idea of how to do it. They were excellent at "furthermore", but weak at "on the other hand". As he says,

Children may exhibit little critical thinking in school, not because they are incapable but because they have little opportunity to do so.

(Ibid., p.10)

This book aims to explore not only the opportunities for extending writing and providing a breadth of writing experience with young children but also the view, beginning to be shared by several researchers, that far more needs to be done with young children not only in terms of looking at the product, but also with respect to process. Our first chapter deals with this point and highlights much of the research currently being carried out in Canada which suggests that writing be viewed as a 'problem-solving process'.

We agree with comments made by the authors of the Sheffield Writing at the Transition project (SCDC 1986) that:

writing in schools (both primary and secondary) is stuck in a rut. This rut has characteristics that are to do with a limited range of purposes and types, a uniformity of ways in which writing is initiated, a lack of variety in the ways writing is related to teaching and learning and, finally, a failure to offer pupils experiences of writing as a process.

Indeed, as the bond between writing and learning is inextricably interwoven, we agree with the Sheffield team that the purposes of writing should not be limited to drill and practice exercises or the simple retelling of information learned etc., but rather should be to help all children to:
–   organise themselves;
–   give shape to and develop their thoughts;
–   work on and give meaning to their experiences and feelings.

So often teachers feel the need to devise or create an unusual, often artificial experience to stimulate imaginative and qualitative writing with young children. Chapter Two aims to draw upon the natural links between writing and media education in an attempt to illustrate how natural such stimuli can be. Media education in the primary years is valuable in its own right but the genuine opportunities it provides for young children to write and express opinions in written form warrants its serious consideration in any discussion of the development of children's writing.

Chapter Three tackles the issue of publishing in relation to children's writing. Publishing seems a natural extension of the writing process and, as word processors become more widely available within the primary classroom, we felt it was necessary to include discussion of the wider issues involving both the strengths and limitations of such equipment.

Chapter Four looks particularly at the principal aims of writing as identified by Kinneavy (1971). Included in chapters on literary, expressive, persuasive and referential writing is a series of case studies which shows how such writing can develop in the primary school when the purpose is genuine and the teacher is prepared to follow the interests of the children. The message throughout the book is clear: when a writing task has real purpose and meaning to the children, their involvement is genuine and their work will show greater depth of understanding and expression. We believe that opportunities for breadth and variety in writing should be given to all children and not withheld from low attainers who are often presented with narrow, structured writing drill and a limited range of purposes. All children should

be offered a wide range of purposes and modes of writing that are meaningful, relevant and genuine.

Clearly, writing is a problem-solving process. We must be aware of the notion that:

> it is entirely possible to read about children, review research and text books about writing, 'teach' them, yet still be unaware of their processes of learning and writing.

> (Graves 1984)

Developing an awareness of process is an enormous task especially considering all that is involved in writing. Children's writing, we are told, is affected by:

> many variables, most of them unknown at the time of the composing process. Children write for unique reasons, employ highly individual coping strategies, and view writing in ways peculiar to their own person. In short, the writing process is as variable and unique as the individual's personality.

> (Ibid., p.40)

We accept this and have aimed to demonstrate the importance of a creative teacher–child relationship within the classroom and an atmosphere that supports children and encourages the sharing and expression of personal thoughts and opinions. Teachers must respect the complex nature of the composing process if writing is to become a collaborative affair where they help children to perceive themselves as writers, and find a way of demonstrating the uses of writing.

Equally important as a means of eliciting good writing must be the genuineness of the task. Our message throughout the book is that in the school situation there are opportunities where there is a real need to offer a persuasive argument or which allow children the freedom to express personal opinions and concerns and these should be seized upon. An anecdote may serve as an example of this point. One child brought a hedgehog to school and said he was keeping it as a pet. This rather distressed a teacher who told the child he should let the hedgehog go, and explained to all the children his reasons for saying this. All the class had strong opinions and became emotionally involved, with the result that a wonderful opportunity presented itself for persuasive writing. The children were asked to 'prepare their case' in readiness for a debate on the rights and wrongs of keeping wild animals as pets. A sense of audience was already established, as was a realistic need to write. Such genuine reasons to write can occur daily in schools whether they be the discussion or arguing of views similar to the one outlined or the writing of cards and letters to people and the need to find and share information. Indeed all the work highlighted in this book has grown from a genuine reason for writing and the teacher should be aware of and encourage situations where genuine purposes present themselves. When children have a real need to write then they will write with interest and enthusiasm.

It is evident from the growing research that the emphasis in children's writing is now beginning to swing from the product to the process and the traditional situation of children writing and the teacher reacting is being called into question. We are aware that many factors can affect the writing process, for example the importance of reading and oral language, and we feel that there

3

is a real need to co-ordinate the cognitive approach with both the emotional and imaginal ones.

Throughout the book we are conscious that the writer's feelings should be respected and composition should not be seen as something that can be wrong. Indeed, it can only be seen as unfinished. We see the teacher's task as helping children know what they know. This requires an environment where the creative pupil–teacher relationship exists, encouraging the children's personal growth. Chapter Three on publishing children's writing aims to show the importance of group conferencing and redrafting as part of the writing process. The teacher's role as facilitator and trusted friend is crucial here and is discussed not in terms of responding to children's written texts as products, but as contributing to the whole process being undertaken.

The case studies outlined in Chapters Five to Eight have grown from the children involved, from their interests and from a definite need to write identified by the children themselves. We are not suggesting that the teacher should never assign the written topic to children, however; it is easy to see how this reasoning could be a reaction to the traditional convention of teachers telling children what to write all the time. It seems to be a question of getting the balance right in order to achieve real needs in the teaching of writing. As Donald Murray suggests (in Graves 1984),

you can't write about nothing. Yet everyday students in thousands of classrooms are asked to write about nothing. They are asked to write about experiences that are not theirs, or if they are, to write about experiences long since sterile. Still, there is an important place for the assigned topic; it belongs in the writer's diet.

1 Writing as a Problem-solving Process

There can be no question that children do want to write. Observe in any nursery classroom the evidence of mark-making by preschool children. These marks categorically say 'I AM'. In the past the major studies on written language have been mainly concerned with older children, and have based their findings on texts produced by them. As a consequence, the results of these studies have been 'text based' as opposed to 'writer based'. This is because it is not easy to determine the psychological processes which go on inside children's minds and it is much easier to study the product.

Bereiter (in Gregg and Steinberg 1980, p.77) is not critical of researchers who have failed to follow the precept 'look at the process, not the product' since to do this requires a psychological model of the writing process and work in this domain is only just beginning.

The work of Bereiter and Scardamalia suggests that the development of written language should be seen as an adjustment from a language production system dependent upon a conversational partner (i.e. through speech) to a system whereby the writer must learn to function autonomously. They identified three production difficulties:

1. the slow rate at which children write could affect short-term memory loss, i.e. children involved in the laborious process of writing down every word and letter forget what they were going to say;

2. that the mechanics of handwriting compete with the higher level demands of content planning, i.e. concentration on letter formation and the presentation of the work becomes more important to the child than the actual thought and content of the writing;

3. the lack of external signals, i.e. the absence of a conversational partner who can respond to ideas, questions and stimulate further thought.

Viewed in this context, the information processing load seems so heavy that it is a wonder that young children cope as well as they do. Writing is indeed a problem-solving activity. Further research undertaken by Scardamalia and Bereiter (in Martlew 1983) considers the interaction of various cognitive processes during evaluation and revision, in order to gain a deeper understanding of children's competences and limitations in composition. These are:

a) language production
b) evaluation
c) tactical decisions (such as whether to delete or rewrite)
d) executive control of the overall process (allocating resources to the various subprocesses and switching from one to another)

Since writing is such a complex activity, young children have much to master. Young children seldom stop and reflect when generating text to higher levels of evaluation and planning. This may be because they have yet to learn that this is a good thing to do. Another possibility is that their attention is absorbed with the problems of lower-level text generation, for example handwriting, letter formation, spelling etc. to such an extent that this takes priority. Children cannot possibly attend to all the requirements of the writing process simultaneously so, as Scardamalia and Bereiter suggest (in Martlew 1983):

> attention to one thing means neglect of another, and so one can never be sure that a child's failure to do something in writing indicates a lack of competence. It may merely reflect an inability to direct cognitive resources to that aspect of writing when it is needed. This is particularly true of the higher level concerns of writing such as the formulation of plans and goals, attention to audience, and evaluation.

When a written task is set, its purpose must be clear to both the teacher and pupil. If the aim is purely presentational, the teacher cannnot expect high level concerns to be fostered in the writing. Equally, if the teacher is wanting high level content showing deep cognitive understanding and expression, then s/he cannot expect presentation to be at a similarly high level. It is very difficult for children to attend to both features with their respective cognitive demands.

Since writing does take place in the classroom and this activity calls for teacher–pupil interaction, teacher-intervention must play a dominant part in the writing process. Indeed, the practice to be observed in many primary classrooms is that of the teacher intervening with the intended outcome of helping children to learn more effectively. According to Bereiter and Scardamalia (in Glaser 1982) however, what the teacher is actually doing is attempting to nullify some of the problems which young children experience, for example problems of learning to generate text without a conversational partner. They argue that in written composition the supports of a conversational partner are removed and, as a result, the oral language production system cannot be carried over intact into written composition: it must be reconstructed in some way to function autonomously instead of interactively. The implication of teacher intervention, according to Bereiter and Scardamalia (ibid.), is that young children will not be given the skills needed for autonomous writing and that it will encourage dependence upon a system that will later need to be abandoned as the teacher withdraws.

It is also said that children need to learn to activate and search their memory again without the aid of prompts which normally come from conversation. When teachers engage in prewriting activities, they are said to be taking over the job of activating memory, doing for children what skilled writers need to be able to do for themselves. They favour an impersonal kind of intervention or 'executive routine', for example giving children cues 'I had better give an example' or 'What I will do next is . . .'.

A further problem young writers can experience is in the area of planning. According to Bereiter and Scardamalia (ibid.),

> expert writing is characterised by abundant planning – not only in advance of writing, but also during writing as plans are revised and further elaborated in response to discoveries occurring in the course of the composition.

Young children's plans are usually confined to decisions about 'what to say next' and may lack attention to their writing as whole. It is said therefore that they are better at 'local planning' than 'whole text planning'. To address the issue of planning however, it is essential to first consider the importance of script theory and story grammars.

Recent work would seem to indicate that the brain retains some kind of schemata which contain information about common experiences. Shank and Abelson (1977) explain it as follows.

As an economy measure in the storage of episodes, when enough of them are alike, they are remembered in terms of a standardised, generalised episode which we call a script.

Scripts provide forms of reference that help us to remember and to comprehend events we experience. They act as a framework for organised knowledge to which can be added new experiences or information. If young children lack appropriate schemata they will experience difficulties with retention of certain information. For example, when children are required to write persuasively on issues that are unfamiliar, their writing may become halting and uncertain. The implication for learning is that the likelihood of children retaining some information about a given topic can be usefully increased by presenting the information within the context for which there is already an existing script. This problem is not so acute with story grammar. Children acquire story grammars by hearing stories repeated several times, for example *The Dark, Dark Wood*. They become aware of the structure of children's stories since they come to understand the beginnings and endings, characters, plots and story sequence. This experience is said to permit young children both to understand and produce stories. It is accepted that children make plans when writing stories because they possess this understanding and story grammars. They understand the format and vocabulary which characterise stories but what is not clear is:

a) do children possess structured schemata for other genre, i.e. do they possess similar knowledge of format, vocabulary and style which characterise other forms of writing, for example argument, scientific etc.?
b) are they able to use this knowledge consciously in planning?

The Canadian research of Bereiter and Scardamalia (in Glaser 1982) concludes that children do possess a knowledge of genre other than narrative, but they are less certain as to the part it plays in children's conscious planning.

Since the importance attached to planning seems to permeate recent research and since it is a factor which must affect the composing process, it is useful to consider the findings of recent research regarding planning in children's writing. The key point from Canadian writing research is that purposefulness and planning are the largest undeveloped areas in the picture that may one day tell the whole story of what constitutes a process model of writing. Young children are preoccupied with producing writing and it is difficult to identify separate thinking that might denote any attempt to plan. As children's writing matures, however, two problems arise. The children need to find something to write about, i.e. content, and they need to execute the writing. Planning may be seen but this usually consists of lists of things to be included in the piece of writing. They are said therefore not to engage in advance planning. Young children do not think like experts: their primary concern is with content and getting it down.

As suggested earlier, the process of writing is coming to be viewed as a problem-solving exercise, the writing task being regarded as a sequence of problems, each one of which has to be overcome by the writer. Within this, the role of planning helps the child to reduce what must seem like an enormous task to something more manageable. Planning is said to influence the overall effectiveness of the finished product. Planning helps focus on essentials and on setting priorities. Plans tell an individual how to set about solving some of the problems being faced by the writer.

In conclusion, we too believe in the notion that writing is a complex problem-solving process and that there is no single correct way to write. The dynamics of the composing process do not involve merely a simple 'think it–say it' model; viewed from the inside, the model that presents itself involves the tasks of planning, retrieving information, creating new ideas and producing and revising language, components which will react throughout the composing process.

Flower and Hayes (in Gregg and Steinberg 1980) offer two useful thoughts to describe the composing process:

a writer in the act is a thinker on a full-time cognitive overload.

a writer caught in the act looks more like a very busy switchboard operator trying to juggle a number of demands on her attention and constraints on what she can do.

Expressing similar concerns, but put much more simply, children, when asked what they thought they did when they wrote, came up with these explanations.

Bonita (aged 8)	When I write I hardly know what is going on. I think that this is so because my brain is thinking and sending orders down to my hand so I can write. Writing makes sense. It is just like when I am reading. When I read I get so deep in the book that I do not hear what my mum wants me to do.
Martin (aged 9)	(perhaps displaying a 'think it–say it' model) When I write I just think on and then I write it down.
Glenn (aged 9)	When I am writing inside my head goes all quiet inside and I set my mind on one thing even though you do not know. Everything in my head concentrates on just the one thing. When I am halfway through a sentence I think about the next sentence.

Children do often make use of the word 'plan' in their explanations.

Ian (aged 9)	I make sure that the words make a sentence and I plan what I am going to write next.
Natalie (aged 9)	I plan all my words like I put one or two words down and I just continue from there.
David (aged 9)	Before I start writing I plan ahead in my head. I also think about my story, what it's going to be about.
Sally (aged 8)	Once you start writing you cannot stop. I think your brain starts going. It will not stop like a bicycle wheel with no brakes.
Gemma (aged 8)	Things that please my teacher are good work, good ideas, quality work we've done ourself.

Flower and Hayes (in Gregg and Steinberg 1980) identify three constraints on the composing process: the demand for integrated knowledge; the linguistic conventions of written text; and the encompassing constraints of the rhetorical problem itself. Although it is probably unwise to put too great an emphasis on what children say they do when they write, it is possible to identify the three constraints expressed in the children's accounts quoted above. These constraints help to account for the varying degrees of conscious control shown by children in their writing. At the age of nine, they still appear to display a 'look into thy heart and write' technique but, as the authors point out, 'this is often a useful heuristic, but it doesn't guarantee that you will find a ready-made conceptual structure there.'

Planning is a highly teachable strategy. A commonly taught kind of plan in schools appears to be a 'plan to say' strategy, a content plan or simplified abstract version of the final product. Of greater value however is what researchers refer to as 'composing plans', comments which the writer makes to him or herself during the process of writing, for example 'What I'll do is write down a few ideas,' or 'I'll elaborate on this point later.' It is this kind of composing which researchers feel we should be teaching since it seems we have concentrated for too long on 'plans to say' at the expense of other types of planning. Good writers, they tell us, not only make initial high level plans 'to do something', but continue to return to and develop these plans as they write.

Obviously, it would be foolish to say that all writing must be planned, but there does appear to be evidence to support the view that good writers must be able to plan. There has been evidence in our own research that some eight-to nine-year-olds display some of the characteristics attributed to fourteen-year-olds in the Canadian research. Although none of the children in our research indicated their intentions without giving the content (for example, 'my opinion is'), some planning was marked by mature features. One child ticked off each idea as he included it in the text. Some children numbered their ideas and crossings out and arrows could be seen. It was clear from plans that the children intended to write opinion essays and there was still a persistent inclination to produce continuous text but, with encouragement, children can be taught to plan in telegraphic form. In the children's planning there was a close resemblance between notes taken during planning and the texts produced.

Even at the age of eight, mature writers are capable of elaborating notes made in telegraphic form and organising material into coherent persuasive argument. We believe that young children do have the elementary logical operations of planning available to them but it takes the guiding questions of an adult and favourably structured situations for these operations to be brought into use.

In this chapter we have attempted to pull together many of the ideas put forward which are said to affect the writing process. We have tried to underline the need for future research to focus on the process rather than the product in children's writing. We stress throughout the book that if writing has a genuine purpose and the child is sufficiently motivated, many of the composing problems outlined in this chapter can be overcome. We must apologise for the patchiness of this overview but, as Bereiter and Scardamalia point out (in Glaser 1982), a complete picture does not yet exist. What we have at the moment are important pieces but many of the pieces of the jigsaw puzzle are still missing.

2 The Media and Children's Writing

The Secretary of State's proposals for National Curriculum English 5–16 includes the following description of media education.

Media education . . . seeks to increase children's critical understanding of the media – namely television, film, video, radio, photography, popular music, printed materials and computer software. How they work, how they produce meaning, how they are organised and how audiences make sense of them, are the issues that media education addresses. It aims to develop systematically children's critical and creative powers through analysis and production of media artefacts. This also deepens their understanding of the pleasure and enjoyment provided by the media. Media education aims to create more active and critical media users who will demand and could contribute to a greater range of diversity of media products.

(Bazalgette 1989)

We are also told that 'media education, like drama, deals with fundamental aspects of language, interpretation and meaning. It is therefore consonant with the aims of English teaching. In fact, media education has often developed in a very explicit way concepts which are of general importance in English.' (DES/WO 1989b).

An important argument, therefore, for the inclusion of media education in the primary phase is that it represents an exciting context for language development work. If, as teachers, we include books, television, radio, photographs, newspapers in our teaching then we are using media, but we need to do more. We need to teach *about* media. This means that we need to develop a systematic and critical approach to media education. Children need to understand that the media are involved in the construction of events and attitudes, rather than merely presenting them as they occur. They need to know that images convey meaning and that the finished product will have been edited, or adjusted to fit a purpose.

The skills required for media education combine many used in language activity:

disscussion	criticism	comprehension
narration	prediction	reasoning
analysis	hypothesising	decision-making
opinion	recording	reading

Children engaged in media work are often required to work collaboratively with peers. This requires the development of group skills, and co-operation is an essential element of media education. For example, in work on tape–slide presentations the children are required to prepare the text, determine the length of each talkover, select the order of the slides, as well as make a fluent recording. Much drafting, editing and redrafting has to take place and we have seen children excel when placed in this learning situation. They need to develop communication skills whilst producing the presentation which must be clear and confident. Media education allows children to offer ideas and opinions especially when the content of the slides, photographs or video is of a contentious nature, for example dealing with issues such as litter, vandalism, pollution etc.

The following case study is included to offer authenticity to the theory by describing its classroom application. The cross-curricular nature of the study and the way media education fits in comfortably with good primary practice made our project especially successful.

Case study: Using the National Museum of Film, Photography and Television

As part of our school's ongoing areas of study, 'the physical world' and 'people', three classes of seven- to eight-year-olds – 4E, 4T and 4C – spent four weeks each working with the education department of the National Museum of Film, Photography and Television.

The following topic network illustrates the areas covered.

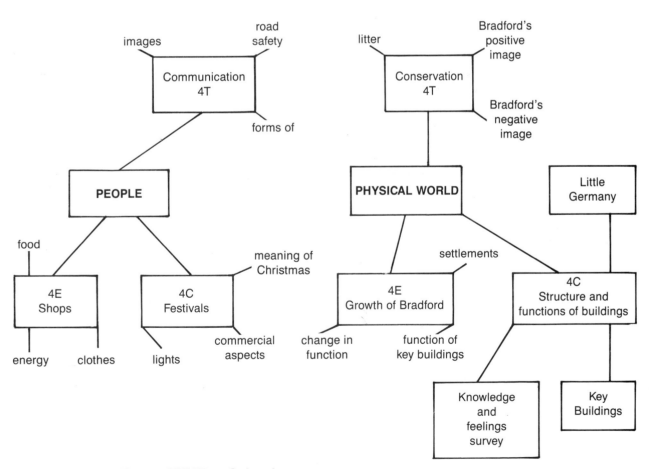

Topic network: Reevy Hill First School

For example, 4T looked at communication, but, within that, three sub-groups were formed to study particular aspects: images, road safety and forms of communication. On the first visit, the children took black and white photographs to illustrate aspects of their investigations. For example, the children studying road safety photographed evidence which communicated the 'rights and wrongs' of safety in the city centre. On the following visit the children printed their photographs at the Museum. Follow-up work in school led to the production of a road safety code using the children's photographs with captions added. This format of taking photographs and developing and printing them was followed by all the groups.

Certain aspects of the work resulted in some excellent learning experiences and involved the children in a variety of situations which demanded very specific skills.

People – the meaning of Christmas

This group of children went armed with cameras and a tape recorder to a busy shopping centre just before Christmas. They wanted to find out the answer to their question 'What does Christmas mean to you?' We photographed and interviewed a good cross-section of the public including an old lady who became upset when she began to tell us Christmas was a sad time for her as both her parents died at Christmas, two teenagers, a Hindu and a Muslim who explained how they intended to celebrate, and a young couple with a one-year-old baby. We met a policeman who patrolled the motorways and who told the children about his worries about drinking and driving and, of course, we interviewed Father Christmas himself. Back in school, the children transcribed the tape and decided to present their findings in matrix form accompanied by a written summary (pp.13-14). The entire project required a great deal of co-operation and the use of many skills including the confidence to interview members of the public and the ability to show sensitivity to the feelings of others, especially the old lady.

Our survey about the meaning of Christmas.

We wanted to find out what Christmas means to people in bradford.

We went into town and made a survey.
These are the results.

things people said / Photo number	birth of baby Jesus	go to church	food	giving	celebrate	enjoy	time with family
1					✓	No its to commercialised	✓
2	✓	✓	dont eat a lot		✓	doesnt like cold weather at christmas	
3	✓	✗	✓	✓	✓		
4	✓	not often	✓		✓	no her parents died at christmas	✓
5		✓	✓	✓	✓	yes has missed out friends	✓
6		✓	✓		✓	✓	✓
7		✗	✓	✓	✓	✓	✓

Our survey about the meaning of Christmas by a group of seven- and eight-year-olds

We asked Seven people what christmas meant to them.

Three people Said that christmas meant the birth of Christ.

Five was on about food but one of the people said she did nt eat a lot.

Three people went to church. Two people dont go to church. One person didn't go to church often.

All seven people said that they celebrated Christmas even though they was not all christmas
Christians

three people thought that christmas was about giving.

Three people enjoy chirstmas But one of these LaDys said enjoy it But missed old friends. one parson side they DiDnt enjoy chirstmas Because its too commercialised. one person said she DiDnt like the cold weather. one more Person said they DiDnt like chirstmas Becaues ner Perents DieD at christmas.

Five People spent time with their family

Writing about the survey by a group of seven- and eight-year-olds

Lights and the commercial aspect of Christmas

Another group photographed lights as a culmination of work on the festival of lights having celebrated Eid, Hannukha, Diwali and Christmas. They wrote poems to express their findings. Here is an example:

tree lights

tree lights

dotted around

Splashes of bright circles

like Splodges of Sparkling diamonds
Shining

Tree Lights by Vicky, aged eight

Other children examined the commercial aspect of Christmas and photographed examples of this. They then researched traditions, using reference materials.

Santa claus

St nicholas helped a poor family. His father didant have enough money foR his daughters to get Married. So St Nicholas helped the father by dropping gold into their Window. In some countries St nicholas is called Santa claus. Santa gives gifts because he is the same Person as St nicholas. At Christmas time Santa gives us gifts today.

Santa Claus by Shaun, aged eight

15

<u>christmas trees.</u>

a long time ago people in England
they used to. have cherry tree's.
because there(they) blossomed. at christmas
it was Prince Albert. qeen victorid's
husband. who. brought. the fist christmas
tree over to england from germany
in 1846 Now a days we all have christmas
trees in our houses to day.

Christmas Trees by Katherine, aged eight

Communication: images

This work was designed to help the children understand or 'read' images presented in photographs taken. Children need to develop skills which will help them make sense of an image or a series of images seen in adverts, on television, in comics etc. One group of children interviewed and photographed a variety of people about their business in the city centre. These included a tax officer, a clerk at the Crown Court, a Rastafarian, an Irish visitor, a police officer and two technicians, a traffic warden and a dress designer. The children paraphrased the interviews and matched the text to the correct photograph as in the following example.

Policemen   Technician's

We met a policeman and two
technicians the techcians make
film's for the policeman They
make road safety film's. The
man at the end is making a
film to help Asian children so
they don't get hurt on the road
The 1st man works as a policeman
the man does not wear a suit
becouse he does not want any
one to see that he is a
policeman. Inside the police
station the policemen watch
Tv and They play snooker and
thing's like that

Interviewing people about their work by Sarah, aged eight

We then decided to ask children not involved in the project to take part in some image analysis. The children were asked to 'read' the images using the photographs, saying what they thought the people did for a job, how they were feeling when the photograph was taken, and so on. Interpretations were compared, and then the children who had taken the photographs gave the real background information from what the interviewees had told them. In this way children shared their thoughts with each other and so began to appreciate that we hold our own personal interpretations. They were developing communication and social skills through the creation and analysis of photographs and information they themselves had generated.

Communication: forms of

Another group took photographs of forms of communication. The aim was to increase the children's knowledge of the nature and variety of the media as a means of communication. We wanted the children to develop their awareness of the influence of media upon their everyday lives. We toured the city centre photographing anything that conveyed meaning. Our collection of photographs included 'say it with flowers', advertising hoardings, signs, the local newspaper building, bill boards and placards. Follow-up work included designing advertisments, shop signs and writing messages.

Structure and functions of buildings

It was decided that the children should explore a recently developed part of Bradford known as Little Germany – itself the subject of recent media attention. We decided

> Reevy Hill School
> Bedale Drive
> Buttershaw
> Bradford
> 23rd February
> Dear Sir or Madam,
> We are writing to you because we have been taking photographs of around the Little Germany area. I am writing about the Paper Hall. Could you tell me when this building was built and any other information about this building.
> Please write back.
> Yours faithfully
> Gareth.

Letter by Gareth, aged eight

to make our own trail of the area using photographs and research from reference materials. We identified on a map where the photographs had been taken and started to collate our research. The children soon became involved in letter writing, asking for information about the buildings and their history. One exciting response came from a Public House. The landlady invited us to bring the children to meet her. She was able to tell them a wealth of information using stories from the past, reference material she had acquired and old paintings and photographs. Gareth wrote the letter on the previous page in an attempt to find out more about the Paper Hall.

He received information and prepared the following caption for his photograph.

The Paper Hall is one of the oldest buildings in Bradford. It was built for a very important man who ruled the area. It is a special building and it is being repaired so that it will look nice again.

Photo and caption by Gareth, aged eight

The children made their trail into a book and the finished product reflected much cross-curricular learning. The development of historical concepts such as looking for evidence and a sense of time were addressed. The children painted pictures of the buildings and displayed them on a time line. Even at the age of seven, the children were beginning to handle historical information. On the next page is a seven-year-old's attempt to make sense of what she had learnt in order to provide a caption for her photograph.

Henry the eigth didnt want the catholic religion in this country. It was against the law to be a catholic. In 1822 the catholic religion was allowed but they did not have a church. Their first mass was in a pub and if they carried on she wood have the licence took off her and she wood not be able to sell any beer. At the time people came to are country for some food because the potatoes in Ireland had gone bad. In Ireland they was a lot of poor people. Some came to Bradford. A lot of people was catholic. In 1876 the church was built. They got the money from the poor Irish people. It was not a fancy church

Writing a caption to a photograph by Katherine, aged eight

The English Key Stage 1 Non-statutory Guidance (NCC 1989) advises how using media education can promote many aspects of the programmes of study in English. These include all aspects of speaking and listening. We are advised that:

children can be encouraged to think of watching television or films, or looking at pictures, as a kind of 'reading'. By looking closely at visual images and discussing exactly what they can see . . . children can begin to see how most still and moving images are organised on purpose, and how visual conventions and symbols are used.

(8.11, C12)

Key buildings

A group of children wanted to find out about key buildings in Bradford and, in particular, what the people who work in them feel and know about them, and what the person in the street thinks about them in terms of architecture and function. We chose the Town Hall, the Interchange, a major hotel, an office block, the Police Headquarters, the Arndale Centre and the National Museum of Film, Photography and Television. This involved the children in tape recording other people's viewpoints as well as having to prepare their questions. Listening skills were important here, as were good clear communication skills and the confidence to carry out the interviews. A gentleman who worked in the Town Hall was able to tell the children much of its history. They listened attentively as he enthused about the building and were left in no doubt as to how he loved working there. The hotel manager, however, was not fond of the modern building he worked in. This feeling was echoed by a secretary who worked in the modern office block. Two visitors to the Interchange did not appreciate its waiting areas and said it was unwelcoming. The project gave the children an insight into issues such as the suggestion that modern architecture does not always offer the best working environment and that historical buildings can be cherished and provide attractive places to work in.

Similarly the group studying Bradford's positive and negative image were engaged in decision-making about what constitutes good and bad. One group had black and white slide film, whilst the other used a polaroid camera. This task addressed issues such as litter, pollution, conservation and economic awareness. The children learnt the different effects that can be achieved using black and white or colour and how advertisers, particularly tourist boards, use light to compose a favourable picture. For example, the Town Hall can appear golden because of the timing of the photograph and the use of certain lenses. The end product was a tape/slide presentation in black and white and a tourist guide in colour. The children were learning to understand that the media is involved in the construction of events and attitudes rather than in the straightforward presentation of them. It seems also that parents have a role to play and we should encourage them to watch television with children and discuss what they see.

The school and the family share the responsibility of preparing the young person for living in a world of powerful images, word and sounds. Children and adults need to be literate in all three of these symbolic systems and this will require some reassessment of educational priorities.

(Unesco declaration of Media Education 1982)

(For further information about media education readers should consult the work done by B.F.I. Education Department, London.)

The project also offered the opportunity to be involved with the developing process. On the next page is how one seven-year-old represented what he did on the project.

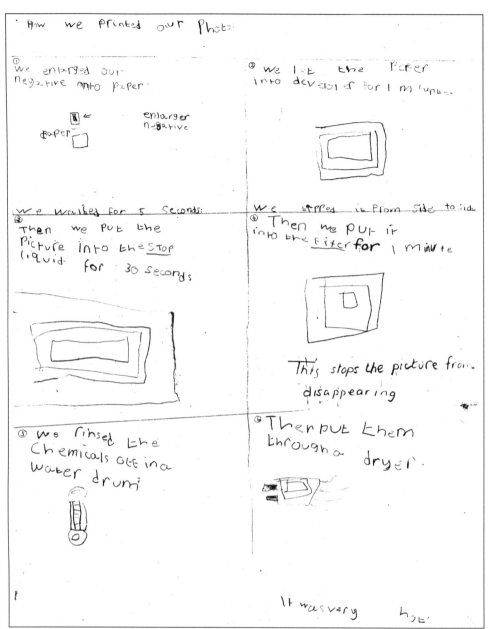

How we printed out pictures by Mark, aged seven

Findings from DES working groups for media education were concerned to stress the importance of the development of attitudes as well as skills. Media education has an invaluable role to play in the encouragement of positive attitudes. These attitudes should include:

appreciation	tolerance
caring for others	originality
co-operation	perseverence
desire to investigate	respect
discernment	responsibility
independence in thinking	self criticism
open-mindedness	self discipline

As primary teachers, we feel we have a responsibility to teach media education. This case study illustrates one attempt to do this since it tried to extend the concept of language learning beyond the written and spoken to encompass audio visual 'languages'.

3 Publishing Children's Writing

The place of published work in the classroom is now well established and the width and variety of materials and resources which should be available is summarised in English Key Stage 1 Non-statutory Guidance (NCC 1989, 11.3, C14).

Classroom display should include: posters, directories, newspapers, magazines, directions, notices and purposeful labels. Children should see their own and other people's writing in different forms: handwritten, printed and 'scribed' in other languages to help them produce writing of greater length, clarity and 'professional' finish.

Ten years ago a teacher we know embarked on a two-term, part-time college-based computer course. She remembers at the time her colleagues asking, 'Why a computer course?' Her answer was twofold. Firstly, since she had responsibility for curriculum development, she thought that in view of the warnings that we were about to enter the new technological era, she ought to become familiar with recent developments. Secondly, she realised that there would be no stopping this innovation and despite the fact that she would place herself well and truly at the creative end of a technological–creative continuum, she ought to at least find out the potential of the computer as a teaching and learning instrument.

A year later, she found herself addressing (perhaps 'pleading' might be a more accurate description) a hall full of parents in an attempt to get them to contribute half the cost of a BBC computer from PTA funds – the other half to be met by the Government. She remembers the antagonism, the scepticism, the arguments for the money to be spent on books instead. At the time her only strong argument in the discussion was to underline the fact that whether we liked it or not the microelectronics revolution was here to stay and we owed it to our children to begin to educate them in this new field.

The introduction of computers to the curriculum was not welcomed without much consideration and concern. Michael Golby (in Garland 1982, p.205) summed up his fears.

I take it as fundamental that we should be concerned with qualitative change in the educational process rather than with the simple addition of new means to old ends or old wine in new bottles. Further to this I think that the essence of education is that it should be concerned with wisdom rather than data, personal perspectives rather than encyclopaedic knowledge.

Echoing his thoughts, two things seemed important at the time. Firstly, it may seem like common sense, but she felt we owed it to the children we teach to explain to them the computer's role in society in these rapidly changing times. We should give them an awareness as to why they are using computers and their potential. Secondly, it seemed that the aims and objectives for the computer must be complementary to good primary practice. Computer education should be integrated into the curriculum, not added on as a 'one off' idiosyncracy to be played with when it happens to be the turn of one particular class.

Ten years later we have seen exciting innovations in the development of software replacing early examples of programs which were of a very low standard, a fact pointed out by Tim O'Shea (TES 1984). He suggested that much software falls down on the fact that:

the teaching program may not be able to respond to different types of conceptual error in the pupils' work . . . Implementing a good teaching program is a considerably harder task than producing a textbook because the program must adapt to the different responses of different pupils.

The use of the computer as an aid to problem solving is not in dispute. The main perpetrator of this approach to be found in classrooms is LOGO, a powerful computer language. Its underlying philosophy is one of seeing children as active builders of their knowledge rather than passive learners of facts. The emphasis is on the process rather than the product. When it comes to 'publishing' results of children's problem solving this can take the form of taking a hard copy of their program for reflection and, if necessary, improvement. They can obtain a copy of the results of their programs in the form of the paths traced out by a Floor Turtle, an output device with wheels whose movements can be controlled by a computer, or simply the path traced out by the pen on the screen which can be dumped to obtain a print-out.

One use of the computer which is proving exciting is its role as retriever of information. In this emancipatory mode children are able to input material and call up facts. A database can provide a teaching tool which will be of use in stimulating discussion, encouraging creative writing and for use in topic work. Demands made on children include decisions as to which headings would be most useful, the use of reference books, ordering of information and consistency. Once the file is created, children can begin to interrogate it and examine it for particular variables. The resource can be a most useful tool for work in the environment. Indeed, the area of information technology has much to offer in cross-curricular learning.

The use of the computer as a word processor in the primary classroom is providing a creative alternative to the repetitive drill and practice exercises outlined by Smith (1984d) which used the computer without any preplanned sense of direction as opposed to attempting to fit it naturally into established philosophy. The computer, when used as a word processor, can offer exciting possibilities for writing. Papert (1980, p.31) tells us that the computer can offer:

children an opportunity to become more like adults, indeed like advanced professionals in their relationship to their intellectual products and to themselves.

This book stresses the importance of children understanding the writing process. The process of creating ideas, planning and revising should be as important as the text itself. This inevitably means altering first drafts and rewriting in order to produce a neat finished copy. Most teachers know how off-putting and frustrating frequent requests of this nature can be. If, however, research into children's writing development is pointing us in the direction of looking behind the words on the page, then the word processor has a valuable role to play. We should be clear that we are working on two facets of education: the computer as a tool and the writing process. Peter Heaney (TES 1984, p.52) suggests we should be clear about our aims.

It was assumed that the word processor of itself would motivate the children to want to use it and that they would move from wanting to use the technology to write, to a position of wanting to write using the technology as a tool to facilitate their own writing.

As far as the writing process is concerned, the task of drafting and reviewing is said by Roger Beard (1984, p.143) 'to warrant urgent attention by teachers and researchers'.

We need to know much more about the ways in which children might be helped to become writers by doing what skilled adults often do – they draft and redraft. The use of word processors may prove to be a help in this.

There seems to have been an insistence on 'fair copies' from the start and that to have to redraft or cross out was often seen as the work of an amateur. The use of a word processor can enable children to receive a finished copy of their thoughts committed to paper without the tedium of laborious rewriting with pencil and paper. Creativity is not stunted by the mechanics of production. The children are offered choices as the production of the poems on the opposite page illustrate. Alexia, aged nine, was able to 'play around' with words. She saved her initial draft and, at a later date, redrafted the poem to produce the finished product.

Most children enjoy using the word processor and the opportunities it presents for collaborative work are enormous. Recent work in desk top publishing has added an exciting dimension to the primary curriculum. Stories or articles for 'copy' can be created, saved and edited at later date. In this way, children create reading material for other children to read. The reading will be meaningful, written in natural language with structures that resemble their own. Collaboration becomes easier with the computer, and joint authorships can be embarked on. Teachers can share in the composing process with children in a much more meaningful way than by simply marking written work. Work with computers offers an opportunity for creative, purposeful discussions about language choices. Hopefully, children will come to see the relationship between language and thought. Communicating ideas through spoken and written language is using language as a vehicle for thought.

It would be foolhardy to pretend that children can learn this skill overnight. Much teaching needs to be done if this medium is to be effective, particularly work on keyboard skills and the editing facility.

A word-processing program in the classroom has the potential to alter the way in which children approach the whole business of writing, but children must always have access to a print-out of their work. Although the word processor allows text to be revised and corrected easily, we must be careful not to make the task a far more laborious process than it would otherwise be. HMI policy documents stress the part that redrafting has to play in promoting good writing and enthusiasts claim that redrafting should play an important part in every classroom. Concern has been expressed, however, that the fair copy is often less well structured and less clearly expressed than some previous

Black is frightening black is
nice sometimes it makes me
think of creepy crawly rats
and mice and when it gets
near the jet black night that
jet black feeling gives me
quite a fright, then again
black can be nice well at
least I know it can be kind to
wild rabbits and mice but I
still can't get the answer to
the problem why sometimes
black makes people cry and
although you wouldn't think so
black makes me feel mad but
sometimes it makes me think
of old old crows who have
travelled the world and have
seen a lot of wonders in their
time but all together I think
black is quite a pleasant
colour so that's fine.

Black is frightening black is nice

sometimes it makes me think of creepy crawly
rats and mice

and when it gets near the jet black night

that jet black feeling gives me quite a fright,

then again black can be nice

well at least I know it can be kind to wild
rabbits and mice

but I still can't get the answer to the problem
why

sometimes black makes people cry

and although you wouldn't think so

black makes me feel mad
but sometimes it makes me think of old old
crows

who have travelled the world

and have seen a lot of wonders in their time.

But all together I think black is quite a pleasant
colour
so that's fine.

Draft and finished poem by Alexia, aged nine

versions of the same piece. We must take care not to place the emphasis on the process of redrafting at the expense of meaning because of a concern to introduce the word processor. As we have seen, the composing process is very demanding and we must make sure we help the children to cope with the additional demands we are asking of them. The value of the word processor cannot be denied, but the technology must not force us to require every piece produced to be redrafted. Some kinds of writing do not lend themselves to this process and I have often seen the look of horror on children's faces when it is suggested that the work could be improved, even when this is done by the most sensitive of teachers.

Adults find they cannot compose directly into a word processor initially. They need time to acquire this skill. So it must be with children. Using the computer as a word processor could be seen as serving a liberating purpose since it reduces the workload of the pupil. I feel it could be argued that the computer does have a role to play, given an understanding of the pragmatics of the classroom situation and the resource implications, if we ask the following major questions at primary level:

● is it of value?
● how worthwhile is it?
● are we able to justify its existence?

We should, however, be aware of disadvantages associated with drafting and word processing as well as the advantages already discussed.

Advantages	Disadvantages
Motivation	Requires keyboard skills
Creativity	Availability
Pride in finished product	Classroom organisation
Ease of experimentation	Impersonality
Negates problems with handwriting	Loss of confidentiality
Neatness is not a problem	

Children need to understand why a piece of writing needs to be reworked. If the criteria are understood by children, then they are less likely to feel frustrated or defeated at the prospect.

This highlights the question of teacher-intervention. Children need much support from a guiding adult; they need to feel confident and free to experiment with writing. They also need an adult or peer with whom they are able to discuss the text and from whom they can receive constructive feedback. If they are secure with the task then they will take more responsibility for the production of their writing. In order to help them we need to be aware of their processes of learning and writing. As Donald Graves (1984, p.40) explains, this is a difficult task since children's writing is affected by 'many variables, most of them unknown at the time of the composing process'. If a creative teacher–pupil relationship exists, the teacher will respect these complexities and writing will become a collaborative affair in which teachers help children to perceive themselves as writers, and in which they find a way of demonstrating the uses for writing.

One very appealing way of conducting this approach in the context of the classroom situation is to hold writing conferences (ibid., p.49). These conferences are founded on a philosophy that treats learning to write as an ongoing, personal experience. Several factors influence the thinking behind the practice in teacher–pupil conferences. The teacher seeks to elicit information from the child as opposed to merely referring to errors. There are two reasons for this tactic: firstly that children need to hear themselves offering opinions – in this way they gain a sense of voice; secondly, from hearing the child speak, the teacher is able to gain a sense of his or her logical thinking and interests.

It seems to be a question of getting the balance right in order to achieve real needs in the teaching of writing. The use of the word processor has helped in the shift of emphasis from paying attention to the mechanics of writing to an understanding of the process. But what part the teacher plays in this process is still open to much more research.

Bereiter and Scardamalia (in Wells and Nichols 1985, p.105) sum up this dilemma very well:

As Vygotsky emphasised, the role of the adult in promoting learning often consists of taking over part of a complex process and then gradually transferring it to the child, as the child grows in competence. But what parts of the writing process to take over, how best to transfer them to the child, and when – these are questions that require quite penetrating research to answer.

Although a word-processing program is one which allows text to be manipulated in a variety of ways, enabling users to edit, store and print text directly into the computer, its use as a means of making language, written in the traditional way with pencil and paper, look more 'professional' and presentable cannot be ignored. Indeed, many of the examples included in this book have used word-processing software called FOLIO (Tedimen Software 1986) in order to offer a 'published' product.

The program enables children to 'rub out' without any obvious marks, it enables children to experiment with the format they wish to employ and they see themselves as 'real writers'.

One disadvantage could be that writing on a screen is on full view for anyone to read. On the one hand it provides opportunities for collaborative writing, but on the other it can inhibit children in their willingness to experiment. It could prove unhelpful in the production of personal writing. Until lap-held computers become the norm in every classroom we must continue to respect the privacy of children if they so wish.

Publishing can appear in other forms and children become skilled at presenting materials in a variety of ways. The examples which appear on the next few pages illustrate a wide range of published texts and the many forms in which they appear.

The excerpt of work on p.30, produced by Nicola, aged five, represents a retelling of the fairy story *Hansel and Gretel*. With the aid of *Fairy Tales* (Resource Publications) she was able to illustrate her story. She felt proud of her finished book and it took its place on the library shelves for others to read.

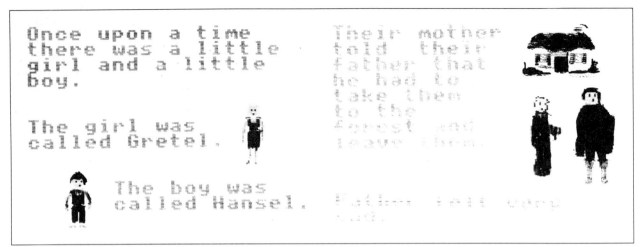

Hansel and Gretel by Nicola, aged five

Our reception children are privileged to enjoy a stimulating role play area which changes to fit a particular area of study. The teachers wanted the children to do some work on mapping skills. We have found that literature can hold the key to introducing many concepts. The story of Little Red Riding Hood lent itself excellently to work on maps and routes as well as stimulating the children's imaginations. The role play area was turned into Grandma's house and the children dressed up and enacted the story many times. One child asked her teacher if they could 'do a play'. The teacher agreed, but asked the children to direct it. The finished product was photographed and videoed, much to the delight of the children who felt important seeing themselves on television. The photographs were used as a stimulus for the children who retold the story.

The children went on a walk around the estate again to reinforce the concept of mapping. This time their 'map' took the form of a huge collage on the wall, made using painted roads and paths, and 3D models of houses and shops. Labels signified particular landmarks, notably the children's homes.

The poem on the opposite page by Emma, aged eight, shows how the word processor can be used to add the 'professional touch' combining art and poetry.

The word processor can, in some cases, help to alleviate the embarrassment of the child who finds extreme difficulties with spelling. On p.32 are two poems written by two nine-year-olds. The poems were typed for inclusion in the school magazine. Zoë's poem had almost all the spellings correct and was very legible in its handwritten form. Heather's poem was undecipherable except to her teacher who had come to understand her idiosyncratic spelling patterns. Both poems are successful in this published form and the reader's attention is not diverted away from the meaning because of the production problems Heather experiences.

The poem on p.33 resulted from the whole class contributing ideas. The brainstorm was written up on a flipchart and then handed to a small group of children to rearrange and edit. This is the finished offering of a group of seven- to eight-year-olds.

A poem produced on the word processor by Emma, aged eight

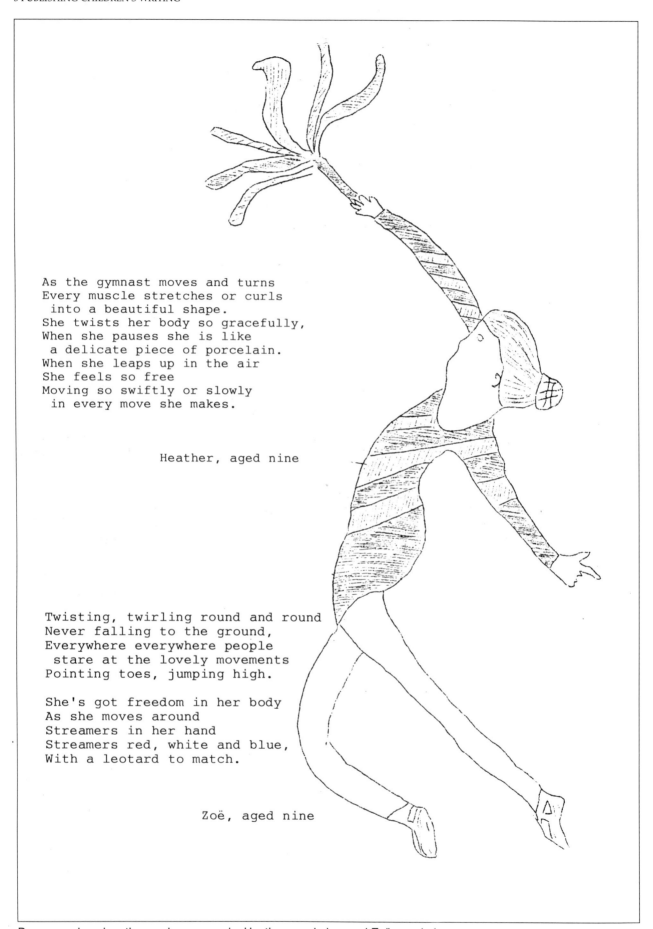

As the gymnast moves and turns
Every muscle stretches or curls
  into a beautiful shape.
She twists her body so gracefully,
When she pauses she is like
  a delicate piece of porcelain.
When she leaps up in the air
She feels so free
Moving so swiftly or slowly
  in every move she makes.

                Heather, aged nine

Twisting, twirling round and round
Never falling to the ground,
Everywhere everywhere people
  stare at the lovely movements
Pointing toes, jumping high.

She's got freedom in her body
As she moves around
Streamers in her hand
Streamers red, white and blue,
With a leotard to match.

                Zoë, aged nine

Poems produced on the word processor by Heather, aged nine, and Zoë, aged nine

```
THE WITCH·


A crooked hat hiding
Green slimy hair
Straggly hair, frogs in there
Hiding black and orange spiders.
Black long nose like a carrot
Sticking out against a face of green mud-like slime
This bloodshot beauty glows in the dark
Eyes like toilet roll middles, cylindrical.
Sharp iron teeth and a tongue like meat
With warts covering her bright red lips
Through her fangs she gives a snake-like hiss.
Horrible laugh, as if she's laying an egg
Black patched cloak and green checked stockings
Never gets a wash or bath
She doesn't care
Sits round the cauldron and makes swirling mists
Putting evil curses on boys and girls
And laughs to herself the whole day and night
```

'Brainstorm' poem written by a class of seven- to eight-year-olds

Children enjoy illustrating their writing as Melanie's, aged eight, accrostic poem on the next page shows us.

James, aged eight, used blue, red, green and yellow pencils alternately to capture the colours depicted in Ted Hughes' story *The Iron Man* (p.35) and felt the need to include 'him' in the presentation.

By asking children to retell a process, for example how a potato crisp gets into a packet, we are able to understand how well they have comprehended what they have learnt. If children are allowed to illustrate their writing, recall will be greater since they are also imagining the event.

The examples shown in this chapter represent pieces of writing which were satisfying to their authors when they completed them. They do not necessarily portray excellence, but they are used here to show how children, from the very young to the more mature, are capable of producing a diversity of styles and purposes. They demonstrate a confidence that belies the complexity of the writing task and show that their authors have delighted in producing them.

Occasionally we, as teachers, are privileged to work with children who have a special gift with words. Sometimes we are presented with writing that we know is very special. As the child's journey into literacy continues we are offered more evidence and must nurture these talents. Some pieces of writing deserve a wider audience. What greater accolade could there be than seeing your poem printed in a published book representing Britain's best writing?

The final example (p.36), a fantasy poem written by Andrew, aged nine, achieved that honour. It was published in the *Cadbury's Book of Poetry* 1988.

Accrostic poem by Melanie, aged eight

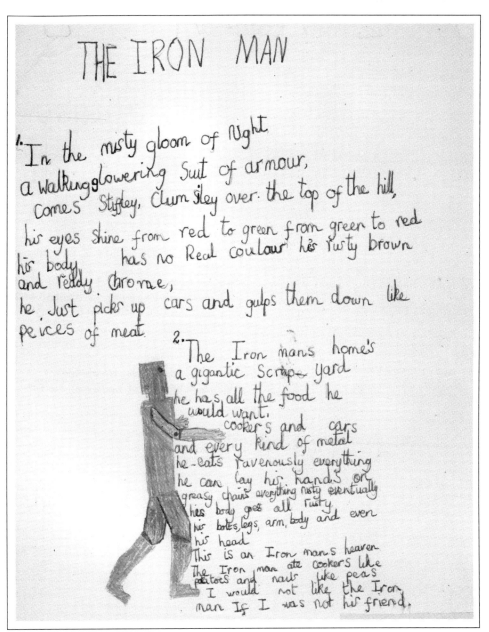

THE IRON MAN

1. In the misty gloom of night
a walking glowering suit of armour,
comes stiffley, Clumsiley over the top of the hill,
his eyes shine from red to green from green to red
his body   has no Real coulour he's rusty brown
and reddy chrome,
he just picks up cars and gulps them down like
peices of meat.

2. The Iron mans home's
a gigantic scrape yard
he has all the food he
would want,
     cookers and   cars
and every kind of metal
he eats ravenously everything
he can lay his hands on
greasy chains everything nasty eventually
his body goes all rusty
his bolts, legs, arm, body and even
his head
This is an Iron mans heaven
The Iron man ate cookers like
patatoes and nails like peas
     I would not like the Iron
man if I was not his friend.

The Iron Man by James, aged eight

Fantasy

The witch of Clignart

The witch of Clignart did no bad,
In fact, the Devil was the only thing that made her
  mad.
She's the daughter of God some people say,
But, more likely a spirit from the land of May.
She built the City of Clignart for the Dukes of
  Champagne
And raised the Pyrenees for a frontier against
  Spain.
Now she lives halfway up the Eiger
With Saladin the frog and Arian her pet tiger.

Andrew Martin (8)
Reevy Hill First School,
Buttershaw, Bradford

Published poem by Andrew, aged nine

4 A Breadth of Experience

In the best traditions of the primary teacher, the teaching of writing has always been allocated prime status in our schools, second only to the teaching of reading. Indeed, historically the preponderance of the '3Rs' has ensured that children have been given both the time and the opportunity to develop their use of the written word. Research and observed evidence in HMI reports (DES 1978, 1982), Bennet *et al*. (1980) and Galton *et al*. (1980) logs large amounts of the school day where children are actually engaged in written tasks, whether they be through the recording of science experiments, working out mathematical problems, the writing of stories or indeed drill practices. Although the recent upsurge of interest and research in the actual content and extension of children's writing is relatively new, its foundations have been well established through a whole series of publications during the 1960s and 1970s aimed at extending and stimulating imaginative and expressive writing development in the primary years. Such manuals and resource banks have been well documented in Beard (1984) and have done much to develop the 'creative writing' phenomenon witnessed during the last three decades.

However, the preponderance of both imaginative prose and factual reporting in primary school writing tasks may not be enough to develop a child's overall writing ability. The Canadian research of Bereiter and Scardamalia highlighted in Chapter One emphasises the importance of providing opportunities for children to write argumentative and opinion essays in schools, but still too few opportunities exist in the primary sector. The work of Britton *et al*. (1975) and Kinneavy (1971) regarding the need for balance in writing tasks offered to young children is well established but the range of writing purposes offered in many primary schools is still restrictive.

The development of thought and the extension of writing are very closely linked and, therefore, where a certain form of writing receives a high profile (for example the imaginative story) at the expense of other forms of writing (for example the persuasive or argumentative) then the child's cognitive and writing skills may become imbalanced. This affects his or her overall writing development and ability to meet the many cognitive demands and solve the problems experienced during the writing process. The child could become well rehearsed in the style, structure and vocabulary required of storywriting and may be able to verbalise and write imaginative fiction fluently. However, if then presented with an unfamiliar situation where s/he has to demonstrate a different style, structure and vocabulary, in persuasive argument for instance, the child's previous lack of experience in such a mode of writing may result in a shallow attempt at the presentation of facts and persuasive style. As outlined in Chapter One, where young children develop story grammars through listening to stories, so they develop a structured schema and knowledge of format, vocabulary and style which characterise other forms of writing, through the provision of opportunities to experiment and extend their experience and practice of that style. Indeed, as Frank Smith says, 'children learn to write by writing'. Therefore, opportunities must be available for children to write, experiment and develop their whole range of writing skills in order to cope with the many writing demands they will meet in society.

While there is a case for children being offered opportunities to write for a balanced range of purposes, it would be a retrograde step to formalise this balance and systematically rotate the writing tasks offered to children in order to maintain and monitor a constant balance between them. The best writing is writing that has been generated from within the child and has real purpose and personal meaning. The flexibility of approach, so much a part of primary education, allows for children to further their own interests and fosters this genuine purpose. Such an approach must be encouraged. Indeed, it can be superficial for the teacher to produce a stimulus and introduce it to children in isolation. Writing tasks should be relevant and within the children's experience. Children should be allowed freedom to follow their own interests and make their own choices and, through this, they should be encouraged to devise their own purposes and ultimately be more in control of their own learning.

Within the role of teacher as facilitator, however, there is a place for encouragement, intervention and guidance to stimulate children's thinking and develop their confidence to journey into the unknown as far as writing styles are concerned. This must grow from a creative teacher–pupil relationship as a process of negotiation with the individual.

The Cox Report (DES/WO 1988) is clear in its view that all children should receive the opportunity to write for a variety of purposes and audiences and that it is only through this provision of a broad range of writing tasks that a child's overall performance and development can be witnessed. The *English in the National Curriculum* Statutory Order (DES/WO 1989a) emphasises this point, stating clearly that:

Pupils should have *frequent* opportunities to write in different contexts and for a variety of purposes and audiences including for themselves.

Each form of written task, whether it be a factual account, a descriptive passage or imaginative story, has its own organisational pattern and style, each requiring a different level of thought and logic (Kinneavy 1971). Therefore, giving young children a balanced approach to writing through the provision of a broad range of written tasks, as suggested in the English in the National Curriculum orders (DES/WO 1989a), will provide them similarly with a forum for developing thought on a whole range of issues. Through this, children will be given the skills and developing confidence to use and express their thoughts through the whole range of situations and pertinent issues that they are likely to face.

There is a school of thought that young children do not possess the skills required for persuasive and argumentative opinion essays. Indeed, the research of Wilkinson and others (1986) indicates that young children (i.e. pre-nine-year-olds) find persuasive writing particularly difficult due to an inability to detach themselves from reliance upon two-way dialogue as a means of viewing opposing arguments. The point is made that young children exhibit difficulty in writing arguments against causes that they personally believe in. However, if persuasive writing is approached through dialogue and discussion, and support is given at the point of transfer into written text, then such thought and writing is not beyond the capabilities of the young writer. For such a situation to be reached, however, it is essential that the correct atmosphere and teacher–pupil relationship is already firmly established.

We believe it is wrong to look at the provision of a broad and balanced writing approach from a longitudinal standpoint where children are not introduced to persuasive or argumentative writing until the latter part of the primary years, with the early years witnessing an overemphasis upon the writing of personal news, imaginative stories and factual reporting of experiences in school. We feel it is essential that a broad approach to writing, tied very closely to the development of oral language through open discussion and debate, is introduced to children as early as possible, allowing them to experiment and experience different writing styles and uses of logic. This will help to lay the foundations for the further development of scripts and forms of reference as outlined earlier and to develop children's confidence to use and switch between these scripts depending upon the genre of the task.

If written tasks are meaningful and relevant to the child, then real depth of thought and understanding can be achieved. Young children, given opportunities to write for a variety of purposes and reasons, are able to demonstrate great sensitivity and emotion if the context is realistic and has both relevance and personal meaning. If such contexts draw children into situations where they argue and debate, not only demonstrating personal opinions but equally listening to others, the provision of support will then allow children to summarise and extend these arguments and personal opinions in text form, so laying the foundations for further development of persuasive writing as the writer matures. In this way, when the issue is of real concern and the correct form of support is given, young children are as capable of writing argumentative and persuasive prose as they are of writing personal news and narrative.

The Kinneavy Model

Kinneavy (1971) categories four principal aims or 'modes' of language which collectively cover all situations where language is required. His model (p.40), based around a communication triangle involving the speaker, listener and the context of the communication, specifies the aims of language, whether oral or written, and ties each one with the audience or context as appropriate.

Within the communication triangle, where expressive discourse is essentially from within the writer exhibiting his or her own feelings or anxieties etc., referential writing is governed by the need to refer to reality or some specific subject material, persuasive writing is dominated by the connection with the audience or listener and the important feature of literary writing is the actual words written to communicate. Kinneavy stresses that these four modes of discourse overlap considerably and that it is impossible to have pure narrative or description without the influence of the other discourse modes. However, within any piece of discourse (oral or written) there will be a dominant mode, this being expressive, referential, literary or persuasive.

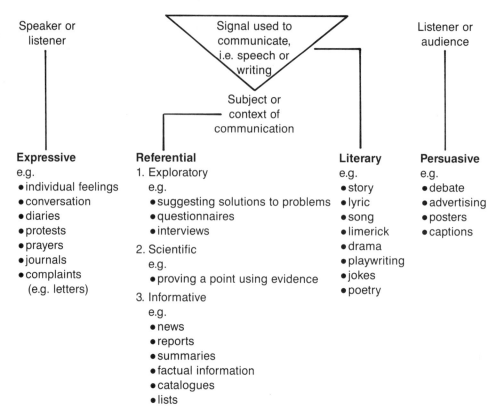

Kinneavy's communication triangle

Related specifically to writing in the primary years, the communication triangle and its associated modes of written discourse are equally relevant as children learn to adapt their line of thought and writing style to the audience and purpose of their writing. If writing tasks encourage a balance between the four modes identified by Kinneavy, the children will develop their ability to switch styles of presentation, structure and script depending upon the situations they meet.

Certain styles do receive natural emphasis in the early years. The influence of children's literature in helping develop story grammars with young children has been discussed already and plays a major part in forming children's earliest writing. Indeed, the writing of narrative using these developing story grammars and related vocabulary will often become the main channel for very young writers because they both understand and become rehearsed in the style of the picture books. As narrative forms perhaps the main mode of writing with young children, so referential writing will often account for the rest. Very young writers are frequently asked to write their news or report on a shared experience. As narrative has its own 'script', so reporting has its own idiosyncratic style. Children realise in such reporting that it is not suitable to begin a report on an experienced event with the words 'once upon a time' and they demonstrate, even at this early stage of development, an alterative structural knowledge of language to the story grammars that become so natural.

The main bulk of written tasks given to young children in the early years do tend to be of the literary or referential kind. Such written tasks do much to give children the confidence to extend their writing in a style that is already familiar to them. However, although the style required in the writing of expressive prose or persuasive argument is different to that required in the writing of story, it is no less important or beyond the capabilities of young writers. It is therefore here that the teacher needs to consciously give children both the encouragement and the opportunities to develop each writing mode's individuality, so balancing the diet of writing demands made upon young children and ensuring a breadth of experience. If introduced sensitively through open discussion, very young writers can and will share personal opinions and emotions and produce reasoned debate if the issue has personal meaning and the environment fosters positive encouragement and mutual trust.

Ample opportunities do arise for teachers to encourage debate, argument and persuasive writing in the classroom without restricting their pupils' freedom or formally structuring writing tasks. Indeed, the use of experiential learning and project work related to first-hand experience in many primary schools provides the ideal situation for the development of a balanced and relevant approach to writing where children are encouraged to question, argue, report and express personal opinion and emotion on a whole range of issues that they have not only experienced but in which they have become deeply involved.

With the correct planning and forethought, most classroom topics will provide opportunities for a balanced writing approach where children have genuine reasons to write. A project on litter, for example, provides children with opportunities for expressive writing in the form of letters of protest or the expression of personal feelings; literary writing in the form of poetry or song, referential writing in the form of surveys, questionnaires, factual accounts and detailed observation, and persuasive writing in the form of designing posters, captions and entering into moral debate. Some children might have particular interests within the topic, for example the origins of litter, alternative uses of waste materials, environmental care or waste recycling. Whatever the interest within the topic, opportunities to develop the four modes of writing can still be provided whilst maintaining the individual's interest and enthusiasm.

The series of case studies given in the following chapters have been highlighted under specific aims of writing: the examples show only a small part of a much larger topic in order to illustrate the response to that particular aim of writing. Invariably, each topic incorporated a balanced approach to writing and although in Chapter Five the devising of a series of storybooks for young children emphasises the literary aim of writing, within the same project writing included reasoned debate on moral issues connected with the characters, poetry, the designing of posters and persuasive packaging to market the books, factual lists of books in the series and profiles of the authors. Examplar material has been chosen to reflect the mixed ability and cultural diversity of the groups involved and is displayed alongside the case studies, valued equally, as it was within the classroom.

The case studies, writing projects and ideas in this book are merely a set of examples that grew from specific interests within the classroom and community, and were undertaken by children aged between five and twelve years. They are not meant to be a prescriptive list or or syllabus to be followed, but an indication of how classroom topics and experiences of immediate interest to the children can be extended to encourage a broad approach to writing and a variety of writing experience whether the children are approaching writing as first- or second-language learners. We hope that the reader will be able to adapt ideas using the Kinneavy writing model to extend and broaden the writing tasks offered to young children in a way that is similarly meaningful and relevant to the individual.

5 The Literary Aims of Writing

Of all the aims of discourse, the literary is the one with which the student of English is the best acquainted (Kinneavy 1971). Indeed, from the earliest days in school, children are offered a diet of writing tasks which emphasise either the literary or referential form: seldom are they given the opportunities to write beyond these aims. Despite the teacher's predilection for offering children tasks within the literary writing mode, it would be misleading to suggest that children become well atuned to the style of all aspects of writing under this umbrella term. Although literary writing involves a number of written forms which include story, lyric, song, limerick, drama and playwriting, jokes and poetry, it is with story that the natural emphasis lies in the primary school. Certainly young children appear to find storywriting more natural than the writing of poetry or song, due in part to the emphasis upon reading fiction in the early years at school. The picture book phenomenon and the lack of factual reference material and poetry in the early readers of most reading schemes help to establish the story grammars that young children employ in their early writing and, therefore, until there develops a true balance in children's early reading, they will continue to approach storywriting naturally at the expense of playwriting, poetry and the other forms.

The influence of story upon children's literary style is so great that even when playwriting or poetry is tackled by young children, the story theme will often permeate their texts. Songs and poetry can often follow a story sequence or emphasise characterisations, so important a part of storywriting itself. It therefore seems essential that in any discussion of the literary aims of writing an understanding of children and their stories becomes a central feature.

As children write stories, they will often try to emulate the emotions and adventures they have already heard or read themselves. However, their actions are rooted in a very complex net of feelings, thoughts and attitudes which must all be considered when responding to children as storywriters. As teachers we should be concerned with children's hearts as well as their minds and be sensitive to what they may be trying to tell us using story as a medium. Children will use the stories they write or tell as catalysts for the telling of personal experiences but we must not forget that they get their experiences from many sources and the world of story and legend plays a big part in their lives. They will pick out elements of these stories and use them in their own way and for their own purposes to weave the material of their own stories, and not merely repeat what they have read. It seems that children use their stories as a means of rearranging life towards the way they would like it to be or feel it ought to be.

When the World was silent and everyone was in bed, the flowers
lifted their heads, their petals looked like skirts and the pollen on
their heads looked like a hat. There was a pretty stream that trickled
passed them all. All the flowers would dance about on the pavements
and then they would go into the house and have a ball.
    Richard woke up. The flowers heard him wake up so they all
dashed back into the garden. He wondered what was happening. He
saw nothing there so he went back to bed. As soon as he dropped off again
the flowers went back in the house and continued the ball. The next
night Richard stayed up and hid behind the table. When he saw the
flowers he was bewildered. He watched them sing and dance and play all
night. The next morning Richard didn't tell anybody what he had seen,
but he went round the garden and looked at the flowers. He noticed that
each flower was in a different place, so he knew he wasn't dreaming that
night.
    The next night he watched them again but unfortunately he
tripped over the chair leg and the flowers saw him and they all ran away
back into the garden. Richard thought he was stupid for scaring all
the flowers away, so the next night he didn't stay up because he knew
that the flowers would not come but instead came a little angel. She
was cross with him for spoiling the flowers fun so she started rattling
the pans and she woke Richard up. "The poor flowers have to stay in
the ground all day and you spoil their fun at night time"! Richard was
very scared and sorry. He promised he would never stay up again to
watch the flowers. The next night he heard the fun but didn't go
downstairs. Soon he looked out of the window. The dwarfs that came
from the garden were dancing around a big fire which crackled. He
thought he had better not go out but one of the dwarfs saw him and
told him to come outside. He slipped his slippers on and put his
dressing gown on, stumbled downstairs and went out of the door. As
soon as he went out of the door the Devil in disguise appeared. "Spoil
the flowers fun - go on"said the Devil trying to make him naughty. "No,
I promised" he said. "Go on" said the Devil. He saw the angel in the
sky telling him not to. She whispered "if you take note of the Devil
you will go down to Hell when you die, but if you take note of me, you
will come to heaven when you die". So he ran indoors, locked the door
and went back to bed and fell back asleep....

Story by Melanie, aged eight

To describe the main elements of the structure of a story as plot, characters, time, setting and mood is not sufficient. A story is an expression of feelings about life. We need to teach children how to structure the stories they write in order to help improve the quality of their work. Certainly, the classical literary theories point to the need for literary writing to conform to established patterns and as landscapes and portraits are judged on their imitation of reality, so novels, short stories and plays are judged by the norm. Therefore, although Kinneavy (1971) points to the central feature of literary discourse as the words themselves, there is still a need for children to understand the established structure of the medium in order to achieve success. Literary writing, traditionally regarded in the 'creative writing' mould, does evoke the feeling of freedom: freedom from constraints and the freedom of creative and imaginative expression. Such freedom in stories, however, can only develop successfully if seen alongside the established and recognised structures already in place.

It is easy for teachers to view storywriting among children as a natural and inevitable consequence of reading fiction but it would be wrong for the teacher to assume that, by reading stories, children will learn all the skills and structures required of them. It is therefore crucial that children are not left to purely drift into story. It may appear to be an easy option for the teacher to say 'go and write a story' but it is questionable whether this would be sufficient to encourage development of the discourse form. Children need to be introduced to the structures by the teacher if their storywriting is to achieve depth and incorporate the detail of character, plot, setting, style, themes, uses of senses, expression of feelings and story beginning and ending. It would indeed be worrying if an older child was always beginning his or her stories with the phrase 'once upon a time'. There needs to be development and it is for the teacher to understand the framework for development and recognise when to introduce guidance to the child and respond accordingly.

Included in the Appendix is a framework for teachers responding to children's stories. It covers the main structural features of storywriting already identified and, although meant to help teachers in their response to children's stories, it also provides a clear guide for the development and planning of children's storywriting towards higher levels of cognition.

The 'literary writing' umbrella is much wider than purely storywriting and although children do turn quite naturally to stories in their writing, it is important that the teacher offers many opportunities for children to develop the other forms of literary discourse as well. Only through this will songwriting and poetry become as natural as narrative. Our case studies have tried to balance the literary aims of writing and show how such writing can develop naturally and be both meaningful and relevant to the children. In our case studies songwriting, poetry and storywriting are seen to develop as separate projects but this is a false impression. Within the literary writing aim there are several identifiable structures, for example story, song, joke etc. but their overlap is huge and all can become entwined. Stories can include humour, song, expressive poetry etc., as songs can include word play and storytelling. The case studies should therefore not be viewed separately but as parts of a whole, the whole being the creative use of language.

Case study: The design of a whole reading experience

Sewing the seed

Following an idea gleaned from a mathematics course on the use of puppets and fiction as a means of stimulating mathematics work with young children, several sets of hand-knitted toys and figures were collected for use with the four- to six-year-old children in school to help with their number work. The three bears with three beds and three chairs, Snow White and the seven dwarfs, ten knitted 'tin soldiers' and Baa Baa Black Sheep with three bags of wool were all introduced successfully as meaningful ways of overcoming number difficulties with young children. Two parents were enthusiastic about the idea and continued knitting and devising other collections for use in the same way. Two football teams were knitted as well as a scarecrow family complete with knitted carrots, mushrooms and cabbages. These were presented to the school along with a collection of ten knitted characters. The ten characters, including a clown, fisherman, artist and witch, proved to have far more potential than at first thought, developing beyond basic number work into a major child-initiated writing project involving children throughout the five to nine age range.

The ten knitted characters were introduced to young children in the same way other puppets had been introduced, i.e. to extend number bonds and number conservation. However, whenever these characters were introduced, the children would make up names for them and enter into imaginative play, devising conversation between them and improvising whole stories. A language support teacher decided to use the characters to stimulate language and imaginative discourse with young bilingual children. The characters were introduced and discussion not only developed names for the characters but whole biographies, including information about their personalities and the relationships between them. Each child took a character and in turn told the rest of the group about it, including its name and its whole history and personality. Enthusiasm mounted as the group became attached to the characters and, after several sessions using them for oral work, the natural development continued and the children wrote characterisations of the figures. These characterisations became far more than visual descriptions, some taking on rather a personal touch as the aggressive child went into detail about the cruelty of the witch and the withdrawn child went into detail about the character having no friends and being very much a loner. The group was of mixed ability so some used Breakthrough Sentence Makers while some wrote independently, but all worked co-operatively to produce a series of imaginative descriptions which were then word processed by the children and teacher, and bound into book form. Illustrations were drawn by the children and the completed series of books were shared among the group.

This imaginative play caught the children's interest and it was suggested by the children that other books could be written and shared, not only between the group but with a wider audience. Stories seemed to be the most popular and so a character was chosen and passed around the group, each child continuing the adventure as the character moved around the circle.

Putting into context

Whilst sharing these books, the teacher extended discussion into related issues, for example, where did the characters live? Were they friends with each other? The children responded with many suggestions, all centred on a fictional village and forest. The characters made up the population of the village and the children were definite in their picture of the village. A river ran through it and the witches' castle stood in the middle of the dark, dark forest. Certainly their ideas called upon the best of their story experience. One girl suggested that a dragon lived in the forest and so this character was added to the collection. Pictorial maps were drawn and the village was given realism including buildings and roads.

The characters were given houses and places in the village and its name was suggested by one child. It was to be called Kallusi Village. It was constructed using plaster and clay and children used the characters and the model for creative and collaborative play. Clay houses were modelled and added to the set and the village became the focus of many stories told and acted by the children and their knitted figures.

Other stories were written by the children involving each of the characters. Once again they were published and illustrated by each author. These latter stories explored the relationships between characters in the village. Gradually the village of Kallusi and its characters became an entwined mixture of the adventure, humour, and extremes of good and bad, joy and sadness that dominates so much of young children's fiction. A collection of twenty storybooks were amassed by these five- to six-year-olds, each showing an understanding of story grammar and deep imagination. They were compared with other published material, as a result of which songs and synopsis were added by some children and author profiles were added inside the back covers of the books. The whole book series, characters and village were left in the school library for other children to share.

Sajid got a stick.

He put the stick by the door.

Storybook by Yusef, aged five

Towards the second phase

The project had been received with developing curiosity by other children in the school. Both young and older children casually picked up the books and read them in succession and the village, characters and their adventures soon provoked great interest. What was the witch going to do next? Would Mr Green find some friends? All kinds of questions were put by the children to the support teacher when he went into their classroom. The project was extended into classes of six- to seven-year-olds at their own request. Stories were extended further and the fiction written by the older children became longer, more complex and moralistic in nature. The rights and wrongs associated with the behaviour of some characters in the stories were introduced. Issues of selfishness and greed were discussed and the stories contained the complex blend of emotions that mark the emergence of advanced storywriters.

Many of the stories were translated into their mother tongue by children and parents. This was felt to be very important in supporting not only the children's developing competence in English but also the development of their mother tongue. Bilingual children are too often seen as being a problem and are not recognised for the skills they bring to school. Several researchers do point out the positive effect mother-tongue support can have upon the bilingual child's overall educational success. Obviously monolingual teachers cannot become competent in another language overnight, but they can value the languages children bring to school and encourage children to use these languages in their work. By encouraging children to use their skills in translating their stories together and involving parents in this, the teacher was giving status to the children's mother tongue. Cummins and Swain (1986) highlights a series of essential steps that the monolingual teacher must make if success is to be encouraged:

a)   the language and culture of bilingual children needs to be incorporated into the school;

b)   the community needs to be encouraged to take part in school in as many ways as possible;

c)   children need to be encouraged to use their home language;

d)   evaluations of children need to alter, avoiding seeing children learning English as a second language as 'problems'.

All four steps had been taken within this project and the whole package has now become a well-used and well-liked series of storybooks in three broad levels according to length, complexity and interest level. They are written in two and sometimes three languages so that they can be taken home by the children and read with understanding by their families.

Page 1.

mrs Wizal the unhappy Witch.

Once upon a time there lived a Kind but unhappy Witch.

She lived in a Vilage but She had no Frineds

Page from a storybook by Asma and Sunita, aged eight

Once upon a time there lived a poor dragon. He was lonely. He had no friends.

Page from a storybook by Atif, aged seven

Postscript

Some of the stories have since been used to stimulate problem-solving activities. How could we help move the tree that fell on Mr Green? How could we trap the dragon without harming him? Intricate machinery and detailed written solutions have formed only a few of the spin-off activities associated with the reading books in the series.

The pack, now twelve months old, is still in use with different groups of children through school and the number of books in the series is still being extended. The characters still evoke imaginative adventures and children still lose themselves in an imaginary world. The stories are read to the class, the characters are used for storytelling and children still readily take up the books, accepting them alongside other published material.

Case study: The Unfriendly Game: an introduction to playwriting

The Bird Garden – A beginning

A class of six- to eight-year-old children, as part of their reading experience, was focusing upon the work of the author Gerald Rose. The children had been introduced to the book *The Tiger Skin Rug* and had shown interest in reading more of Gerald Rose's work. Consequently, a number of books were made available. One group of children particularly enjoyed *The Bird Garden,* a story which explores the jealousy between the favourite birds in the sultan's palace garden when a mynah bird is introduced. After reading the book several times, the children wanted to share the story with a wider audience by acting it out in role play.

The difficulties of this were discussed and examples of simple written plays were introduced to illustrate the need for a script format and the condensing of the narrative to allow greater dialogue between the characters. It did not take long for the children to appreciate the difference between the format of a story and that of a play. The children therefore took the story of *The Bird Garden* and collaboratively began to devise a script that followed the storyline but laid far more emphasis upon the dialogue form. The script took shape and, although certain parts of the story received a different emphasis to the Gerald Rose original, the story was well presented. This script (p.50) formed the basis of an acted version of the Bird Garden story.

The children were encouraged to continue the story-line beyond the point where Gerald Rose ends his book. Suggestions were made and discussion developed as to how the story could continue and then children were left on their own to work out and write their own versions. The resulting scripts continued the dialogue format and maintained the style of the play, further emphasising conflict situations and the arguments between the jealous birds in the garden.

The Bird Garden is moralistic and its underlying theme is that being greedy and cruel to others will end in misery for yourself. This message was used positively by the teacher as a means of supporting the school's antiracist policy and its stand against any form of name-calling.

Following discussion around the cruelty of the birds in the story, a comparison was made with the way humans sometimes behave with each other. Members of the group discussed quite openly how they had been cruel to other children and ways in which people had been cruel to them.

Whilst this discussion was still fresh in their minds, the children were given the freedom to enter into role play and devise a story based upon an incident where somebody was being cruel or selfish. Children worked in groups with much enthusiasm, switching between English and their mother tongue in their dialogue. The teacher was interested to see how the children would develop the story involving conflict and how that conflict would be resolved. The resulting play was clearly based upon a collection of experiences including the child who only wanted to spoil everybody's game, the naughty child being sent to the headteacher and a child being involved in an accident. The mixture of emotions, anger, sadness and a sense of caring that came from the different characters became real as the children took on the characters in the play. After several changes and improvisations, a play began to emerge that followed the conventions of traditional story grammars. It had the good characters and a good beginning, and it developed the spirit of realism. It equally had the bad characters, reached a climax and wound down to a happy ending. The play was recorded on cassette tape and played back to allow time for evaluation and group criticism. Following some amendments, the play was re-recorded and the children collaboratively took sections of the tape and made transcripts in the form of a play script. The transcript was put together as a first draft of the play. This first draft concerned itself purely with the spoken dialogue between the characters in the play. Stage directions, sound effects and other points were added that were non-dialogue.

	The birds begged the Mynah bird to teach them how to talk to the sultan.
all the birds	OH we beg we beg you to teach us How to talk
Mynah bird	OK but I will olay teach three Bird's How to talk today
Peacock and a Mynah Bird	OH OH I'll be frise I ibe frist OK dont panic (said Mynah Bird)
Mynah	OK what do you want to laran to say
Peacock	I want to say I am so beautiful a Bird will come a long and kiss me
Mynah	But Mynah Bird taught the Pecock to say OH sultan your beradisias long an elehane trunk
Cockatoo and Mynah Bird	I'l be second. I'l be second OK dont be silly
Mynah	What do want to say
Colkatoo	I want to say everybody likes me sultan please make me your favourite Bird

Part of *The Bird Garden* script by Shabana, aged seven

Towards stage 2

After the play had been shared with a wider audience, discussion with the group centred around ways of extending it and ways of helping other people who wished to use the play script. How would they know what the characters were like? How would they know whether the story was suitable for them to perform? How would they know where the story took place and where the scene changes occurred?

There were several lines of thought and a brainstorming session highlighted sections where songs could be added, scene changes where further written detail was required and where specific stage directions could be included. It was decided that a list of characters and synopsis of the story could be added at the beginning of the play. Each child chose a task from the list and either independently or in groups began to fill gaps that they had identified.

Perhaps the most difficult task was the setting of the scene and concentrating on the detailed scenery which was required if the play was to be acted with props. The children constructed cardboard backdrops for each scene. Once they were drawn, a description of the scene seemed much easier to write.

All the completed pieces of writing were shared with and edited by other members of the group. Full stops were checked as were spellings and any final alterations were suggested by the children. When the whole group were happy with the work, it was typed and the whole play compiled.

Postscript

Play writing has really taken off in the school now and puppet plays are well established. The school regularly performs plays that have been written by the children. Older children and friends are involved in the translation of the plays into Urdu and Gujarate so that the appeal and meaning of the play reaches the wider audience of parents, grandparents and other community groups, many of whom maintain the use of their mother tongue as their primary means of communication. Children now write in dialogue script form, inserting their own stage directions, and the subjects of their plays cover a variety of themes including adventure, environmental care, and many other issues which have naturally captured their interest.

Case study: The bilingual storyteller

Bilingualism: a place in the classroom?

The question of promoting and encouraging bilingualism and the teaching of mother tongue in the classroom has always been a contentious issue in Britain when the mother tongue is other than English or Welsh. Evidence from the Motet survey (1978-80) in Finbarre Fitzpatrick (1984) and research undertaken by Downing (1984) and McLaughlin (1978) highlights the positive impact which bilingual support and mother tongue teaching have upon the general cognitive development and social confidence of children learning English as a second language. Such evidence is difficult to discount when teachers in schools with large numbers of children learning English as a second language witness the greater confidence, self-pride and cognitive understanding of children when supported and encouraged in the use of their mother tongue. Despite this, the Swann Report (1985) firmly discounted published evidence and general feeling that mother tongue teaching in school helps to overcome the educational disadvantage facing many British-Asian children as they enter a school system revolving around English as the medium of instruction.

It is interesting to note how young children can often pause in their conversation or writing, unable to think of the actual English words or phrases to convey the meaning they wish to express, but can fluently express this meaning in their mother tongue. To recognise, support and value its usage positively in the classroom is therefore far more than a confidence-boosting exercise with children. It can draw the school, parents and community closer together; it can lead to the greater involvement and motivation of the child in classroom tasks and, according to Cox *et al.* (DES/WO 1988, para. 12.9), it can actually lead to children making greater progress in English itself. Not to provide such support surely denies children the right to fulfil their potential.

Deciding the theme

A group of like-minded teachers, working in a team-teaching situation with six- to eight-year-old children having Urdu or Gujarate as their mother tongue, decided to work towards the production of a multilingual play, written by the children, to draw both parents and the community into school, support the children's home language and continue to boost the confidence and self-esteem of the children. The teachers were clear in their view that the support of children's bilingual or multilingual skills would be of clear educational benefit to the children involved. From the outset the teachers made clear their intention to draw older children and parents together to help with the details of the community languages to be used and the group was to establish links with a neighbouring secondary school to write songs and provide tabla accompaniment. The whole project was to be cross-curricular, the children designing and building the scenery, and involving art, science and language work all revolving around the central feature which was to be the production and staging of a multilingual story.

Although the basic idea was teacher-led, staff wanted to maintain a level of freedom to follow the children's interests and ideas, to develop them and perhaps even to change direction if required. The theme of environmental care and the hazards of litter had already received a high profile in school as the area around the school had a major litter problem and there had been several sightings of rats and vermin in the precinct adjoining the school. It therefore seemed natural to build on this as it already formed part of the children's experience in school. A traditional story idea was used that incorporated a mixture of moods and emotions but that allowed freedom in the children's interpretation of the basic story-line. The play was loosely based upon the folk story the Pied Piper of Hamlin. As this form of project was new to the children, it was thought that the use of a familiar tale as a starting point could leave a greater amount of time to the development of the main priority of the project, the multilingual aspect.

Opening discussion

Working in small groups, several children became involved in discussion around the idea of litter and rat infestation. What would the rats do? What damage could they inflict? How would the children feel living with rats all around them? These were all questions taken up readily by the children as they discussed the scenario of a community infested with rats. The rats would bite through the carpets, they would steal and nibble at food, and they would bite the people living in the town. All kinds of suggestions were put forward by the children and role play was encouraged: the teacher was particularly keen for the children to use their mother tongues within the role play sessions as this formed their natural means of expression. Short scenes were therefore quickly devised as children naturally and fluently exchanged dialogue with great feeling and expression in either Urdu or Gujarate. The scenes were then translated by the children and the beginnings of the play were there.

```
URDU SCENE


daykho mairy lerky ka hath choohay nay kati hai
dayhko mairy roti ko choohay kha leeya hai
daykho mairy carpeet ko choohay nay kha leeya hai
ham tang ho ga-ay hain. ham kya kerengay?
ham mayor kay pas ja-engay



GUJARATE SCENE


mahri baby nay oonder kady gya
mahro rotly nay oondera kharoo paree gya
mahro carpet nay oondera kharoo paree gya
may bo thaki geya oondera ha-tay
aspray mayor jo-a ja-y



ENGLISH TRANSLATION


On no - the rats have eaten the carpet. It will
cost a fortune to replace it.
On no, rats again. Thats the third time. We'll have
to throw them away.

Ow! Stop it! Stop it! Oh no, the rats have bitten
my little boy - take him to the doctor's.

We are tired and fed up of this. We have to
go and see the mayor.
```

Short scenes in Urdu, Gujarate and English

Working outwards from these scenes, the sequence and general mood of the story soon began to unfold as several groups of children began to devise other scenes, character dialogue and a narration to hold the whole story together.

The children made suggestions and deviated from the original Pied Piper tale but this was encouraged by the teacher as a means of giving them greater control over the project, including decision-making, role-negotiation, and team-co-operation. Sections of the story which had been written in English by the children were then verbally translated by them into their mother tongue. Children became the teachers as members of staff took on a learning role, they too facing languages other than their mother tongue. Children were keen to contribute ideas and mother-tongue translations. As the teacher transcribed their suggestions, the children questioned certain phrases and words, carefully amending the script and the use of both Urdu and Gujarate.

Parents were involved in checking the mother-tongue sections of the play to ensure that they were grammatically correct. The completed dialogue scripts were then shared among groups of children. They were taken home and shared with other members of the family, developing great interest in the project among parents and the community.

```
Teacher      We have 'listen people to my story' and we have
             got it so far in Gujarate - 'mari tari lisken kero
Anita        No it's not tari its 'wastha'.
Teacher      'watha' how do you know. Are you sure.
Anita        Yes my grandma told me that ....
Teacher      Mari watha - now listen what comes here
all.         hambro!
Teacher      hambro?
all.         yes hambro.
             (teacher writes it down)
teacher      Now listen. It is Mari watha hambro.
Hamida       Hambro. That means 'listen to us'.
teacher      hambro?
             Children nod.
teacher      hambro kero?
Hamida       Yes.
teacher      So we have got 'mari watha hambro kero'
             do we need kero aswell?
Children     Yes
teacher      So it sounds something like this?
             teacher proceeds to sing with guitar.
                 'Listen people to my story'.
             so we've got.
                 'mari watha hambro kero'
             do we want kero aswell. Does that sound right
Anita        Yes thats nearly right
teacher      listen people to my story or come and listen
             to the story. It doesn't have to be exact as
             long as it's similar.
                 'Mari watha hambro ....
Hamida       Hambro thats it.
teacher          'Mari watha hambro kero' Everybody sing it
             all the children join in with the song
                 'mari watha hambro kero'
```

Amending the script in Urdu, Gujarate and English

Children were already used to writing songs as part of the extension of their own story work and therefore the inclusion of songs in the play seemed to be a natural extension. Some sat down in groups and began to write poems and songs to intersperse throughout the play. Others preferred time for personal reflection and the independence of writing in isolation. Some poems had definite rhythmic metre whilst others were more abstract. The children were encouraged to improvise vocal melody, interpreting the words they had written. Some were very successful and conveyed the mood of the songs with great feeling and enthusiasm. Many of the songs were translated by the children with help from both adults and peers and stand as independent literary and musical expressions.

Tabla and percussion instruments were added to the melodies by other children, the words written on large sheets of paper and all ninety children and staff began to learn the songs written in three languages. Urdu speakers sang in Gujarate and our Gujarate speakers enthusiastically learned the Urdu. The whole play and the project itself had become truly multilingual. Pupils from the local secondary school were so impressed by the children's work that they too began to compose songs for the play. These were equally valued by the staff and incorporated into the play, sung and accompanied on tabla by the composers themselves.

54

```
RATS


Rats are here and rats are there
They're here and there and everywhere
Rats are here and rats are there
They're here and there and everywhere

They fight the dogs, they kill the cats
They bite the babes and eat from vats
Rats are here and rats are there
Those rats are everywhere.

Choohay idher choohay udher (Urdu)      Onder atlay oondera that (Gujarati)
Chalker marna saray                     Atlay a-ya nay chay
Choohay idher choohay udher             Oonder atlay oondera thar
Chalker marna saray                     Atlay a-ya nay chay
Kuttay say vo lertay hain               Ayloko kutera hatay leray
Billion ko vo martay hain               Nay beelari nay malakay
Choohay idher choohay udher             Oonder atlay oondera thar
Chochay her teraf                       Oonder ba day chay


Rats are here and rats are there
They're here and there and everywhere
Rats are here and rats are there
They're here and there and everywhere

They drank the milk, they ate the corn
What a scary town of rats
Rats are here and rats are there
Those rats are everywhere

Choohay idher choohay udher
Chalker marna saray
Choohay idher choohay udher
Chalker marna saray
Bachon ko vo kart-tay hain
Khana bhi vo khatay hain
Choohay idher choohay udher
Choohay her taraf.
```

Song in English, Urdu and Gujarate

Enthusiasm heightened as the scenery was built and the costumes made. The play was rehearsed and children confidently took the lead, using their mother tongue and switching between the three languages used in the play with great confidence and skill. None of the audience during the five performances had any difficulty hearing the children. They spoke, sang and performed with great articulation and enthusiasm. Young children who had exhibited difficulty expressing themselves in English, confidently sang and spoke in their monther tongue. Children confident in English and their mother tongue, developed confidence in a third language. Throughout the project the meaning of the words in each language was stressed as were similarities between the languages. Linguistic patterns and sequences were identified and key patterns and phrases explained so that children clearly understood what the words and songs meant. Posters and invitations were written by the children to advertise the play and children used stills taken during the rehearsals to stimulate writing, including poetry, narrative and problem solving, involving suggestions for curing the town's infestation.

Hima was a girl and she was a little girl that had a sore leg and she was knocking on the door because her friends had all gone away in the mountain and she had no more friends Left and she was sad and she called out my friends come back to me Please dont Leave me a Lone Please come back I am all a Lone and I am sad come back She found a pipe and her friends all came back.

Writing stimulated by work on the play by Farida, aged six

After the event

The play had formed the climax of a whole term's work but still lives on six months after the event. Children, now in different class groups, still exhibit confidence in the use of their mother tongue and in their willingness to share ideas and interact with others. Mother-tongue support now features on the school timetable and children are keen to develop their mother-tongue skills and share with younger children in the school the stories which they have translated into the community's languages. Talk surrounding the project is still evident among the children and writing, storytelling and dramatic expression continues with great enthusiasm as the children build upon their earlier successes. The songs are still sung in school and copies of the play on video are on constant loan to families as they share with pride their children's work.

Case study: Songwriting with young children

Although discussion of the role and development of music does not fall within the brief of this book, to consider approaches to songwriting without including music and its influence upon the writer, would be a negation of the important role musical form and structure have upon the formation and composition of the words of a song. Songs are not poems. They are unique in style and character and therefore to treat songwriting in the same way as the writing of poetry is failing to appreciate the unique place it holds in the development of writing.

Recent texts on the development of children's poetry aim at the freeing of traditional rhyme and pattern, which are often felt to restrain the creative flow of the language, whereas songwriting is somewhat governed by the actual pattern and metre we so often wish to avoid in poetry. Indeed, from the earliest days in school, young children are introduced almost entirely to songs that are strongly rhythmical, repetitive and contain many of the contrived rhyme endings that in poetry we wish to avoid.

The reason for this is simple. Traditionally, for a song to be successful the melody and pattern of the song needs to be such that the singer or listener will easily retain it. Repetition either in words or in the music helps establish the song and therefore governs the actual content and pattern of the words themselves. The songwriter is therefore controlled not by his or her own emotions but by the constraints laid down by the music and its need to conform to established taste even before the music is actually written. Indeed, in most cases with young children, the writing of the music follows the writing of the words. Children who have written the words for a song and embark upon the melody soon begin to realise the problems if the words they have written do not conform to regular pattern and metre. They therefore tend to conform to established musical genre they have heard already. Consequently, written songs will often follow this format both for ease of composition and the greater appreciation from both peers and adults.

Baisakhi, Baisakhi is our happy new year
People dance then they go away,
They go to the temple to sing and to pray
On a very special celebration day.

           Waheed, aged eight

Zest is the best, it beats all the rest,
With a hint of lemon it's a taste that's new.
It's clean and healthy, so cheap to keep you wealthy,
It is the soap for me and you.

           Lucy, aged ten

Poems following established metre

There appears to be a general insecurity felt by many primary teachers when faced with the prospect of teaching music in their classrooms. Whether this comes from purely a lack of confidence in their own musical skills or from some deeper self-consciousness, many teachers will try to avoid musical activity if possible and openly deny having any musical skill themselves. However, songwriting should be encouraged and developed as part of a broad approach to writing. Songwriting has a place in every classroom and it is important that every teacher supports it and provides opportunities for the child, viewing songwriting as a problem-solving process and viewing his or her own role as one of facilitator. The encouragement of songwriting need not be limited to the music specialist: if children are given the opportunities and tools to experiment with and are equally encouraged and supported in their work by the class teacher, then the development of style and pattern, which is so much a part of songs, will often follow as a matter of course.

Music is a natural means of expression and many children will quite naturally sing and improvise melodies, humming or singing to themselves. Even young children looking through songbooks will 'sing' the songs as they read although they do not know the melody written alongside. If the environment is right, therefore, for many children a natural extension of this is the vocalisation and improvisation of melody using words they themselves have written. To encourage the use of the human voice as a musical instrument in this way will avoid children struggling over a xylophone, picking out a melody one note at a time. Indeed, there is a close connection between the production difficulties associated with young children composing music and those children face in writing as outlined by Bereiter and Scardamalia and included in Chapter One. To use the voice as a musical instrument gives children access to immediate fluency in the composition and singing of a melody to words they have already written.

Ways of approach

There are several ways of introducing young children to the writing of songs, whether it be specifically through the writing of extra verses for songs already known, new words for established tunes or the writing of new words and the composition of new tunes to accompany them. Whichever approach is adopted, when the task is well defined and the children understand what they are doing and its relevance, then the response will often show greater concentration among the children concerned. To encourage group co-operation in such tasks will often provide 'in-built' self-appraisal and self-criticism, children suggesting ideas, making choices and then collectively developing the self-confidence to perform and redraft the work being undertaken. Children working in isolation will not have the support of the conversational partner and may become so immersed in their own views that they cannot see other ways of resolving problems.

The need for relevance and meaning is perhaps why the writing of Christmas carols during December seems to generate real imagination and sensitivity from young children. They become involved in the atmosphere of Christmas, they hear songs and music around the Christmas theme constantly and therefore, not surprisingly, they begin to emulate the atmosphere that grows around them.

Similarly, from the earliest years, children begin to identify the close connection between story and song. Nursery rhymes tell simple stories and the majority of songs learned during the primary years are story-based, developing a story theme through each verse of the song, for example 'There was an old woman who swallowed a fly', 'When Goldilocks went to the house of the bears' etc. Many of the radio music broadcasts for schools and many of the short musicals written for use in schools

```
Snowflakes are falling, are falling on the ground
Children are playing, are playing all around.
Snow, so crisp and white, spreading through the
                                    winter night
These are the signs of Christmastime.

Christ was born in a stable bore so long ago.
Wise men brought gifts of Myrhh, Frankinsence and gold.
Shepherds brought their sheep with wool to keep him
                                    warm.

These were the signs of Christmastime.

Christmas comes once a year while winter lasts
                                    much more.

The old lay in their beds keeping warm behind their
                                    door.
Poor and all alone with little food and little wine.
Are these the real signs of Christmastime?
```

The Signs of Christmas, a Christmas carol by Joanne and Ellen, aged ten

develop a story, interspersing it with songs at appropriate points. This experience of musical story, so common in the primary years, helps reinforce the bond between the two elements and provides children with a natural vehicle for the development of songwriting. Children see how songs develop the characters, the scenes and incidents within a story. If this process of extending stories and imaginative prose is taken further into the children's own written work, by encouraging them to extend their own prose with the inclusion of short songs and musical sequences, the story takes on a new importance to the child. Indeed, some of the best songs written by young children are those which grew from personal and imaginative story ideas.

The writing of songs which are isolated from the story or shared experience, for example a major festival such as Eid ul Fitre, Diwali, Baisakhi or Christmas, is more difficult to introduce. Personal songs and the expression of inner feelings do form an important aspect of songwriting but the writing and singing of such songs often seem alien to young children. Children need both time and encouragement here to experiment for themselves with ideas and feelings. Opportunities need to be made available where children can write expressive songs based on feelings rather than narrative. It is only through this, the writing of persuasive jingles, advertisements, individual songs for assembly, songs about personal feelings and perhaps the emulation of messages and songs produced by the children's own pop idols, that many children are freed from the inhibitions and constraints associated with traditional nursery rhyme and infant song pattern and metre, patterns and styles which hold such a tight influence over our children.

By encouraging children to experiment and giving them both time and patience, the teacher will help them to develop the confidence to express themselves in their own chosen style and not in a style they are forced to emulate.

```
TRAVELLING BACK IN TIME


Travelling back in time
through life's emotions
Swords and shields gleaming in the night
Passing centuries as they fly round us
Don't know where my journey's gone

Chorus   Magic woman take me on,
         So that I can be yours.
         Till I next find my resting place
         next to you yes, face to face

I'd like to fly, be like an arrow,
like a bullet through the night
Steal from the rich give to the poor
So you can fight for a good life

Chorus   Magic woman etc.

Through the rooftops flys somebody,
Stopped the force at Stonehenge,
Saw some druids worshipping the sunlight
Ancient relics all around us.

Chorus   Magic woman

Now my journey is completed
It's time to face reality
The world's out there, go and get it
or you may as well forget it.
```

Travelling Back in Time by Daniel, Michael, Neil and Christopher, all aged twelve

Case study: Poetry from experience

Although the writing of expressive poetry did feature among the creative writing movement in the 1960s and 1970s, little real guidance was ever offered to teachers in the actual development of poetic expression. The teaching of poetic expression is still an idea that receives little attention from researchers and educationalists. Brownjohn (1980 and 1982) has tried to open discussion on the subject and introduce teachers to the variety of poetic forms available, but the majority of literature on the subject either assumes that teachers know how to develop poetic writing already, or follows the general trend set in other forms of writing that 'more of the same' will lead to children developing a deeper understanding of the discourse form and continuing its development. Certainly children do learn to write by writing, but the teacher needs to know how to extend children's writing experiences so that opportunities are developed for them to take on an increasing number of higher level concerns in their writing.

Poetry is a very personal expression of feelings or an interpretation of an event and, as such, children's poems must be valued for their individuality and use of language. There have been moves to free poetry from the contrived rhyme endings and encourage the experiment with words and language. Through this, children are freed from the poetic constraints determined by the strict rhyme and metre that so often restrict the true expression of language which surely must be our aim as teachers. It is difficult to do this if children have limited experience of reading poetry. Perhaps over-indulgence in singing, characteristic of so many primary schools, helps maintain this influence, strict rhyme and metre often being the dominant feature of songs. To override this influence, it is essential that young children are given a massive exposure to different styles of poetry, written by a variety of people including children themselves. It is perhaps in this area that the teacher can positively help children in the development of poetic expression. There seems to be a lack of poetry reading in our schools which must surely be addressed if this form of writing is to develop in the same way storywriting develops with our youngest children.

As with other forms of writing, children produce the best poetry when they have something to write about. The personal or first-hand experience provides an excellent opportunity for children to express themselves poetically but, although the teacher's role is essential in the provision of stimuli and help to the child, he or she must not over-direct: children should be given opportunities to write purely for themselves. In the development of poetry, these opportunities provide children with the freedom to experiment with words in the knowledge that their experiments will not be judged as being either right or wrong. If approached in this way, young children will, through poetry, be encouraged 'to speak of their condition' – presenting their own views of the world and using their 'best words' in their 'best order'; using language 'with the greatest possible incisiveness and power' (DES/WO 1975, 9.22).

As children grow and develop their confidence to share personal thoughts and feelings in poetry as in any literary writing, there is a real need for sensitivity on the part of the teacher. The teacher's role must be that of a trusted friend when discussing personal and emotional statements with young writers. Such writing may have been tentative and will have been the culmination of much thought, debate and reflection on the part of the child. Therefore,

The teacher's response to any serious piece of writing must always, in the first instance, be an accepting one.

(Green 1986)

Children produce the best poetry when they are honest with themselves and open in the expression of their innermost feelings. Certain stimuli, including many of the ideas brought out in the creative writing movement of the 1960s and 1970s, and more particularly that of the first-hand experience, do seem to evoke higher levels of imaginative, exciting and deeply expressive language in children and it is important that these are used positively and children encouraged to recreate the moods and emotions of their experiences using words freely without the constraints of written prose, for example sentence structure etc., which may disturb the flow of their thoughts. Creative play with words will often unleash the child's real feelings, often showing maturity, sensitivity and perhaps opening a window on to the child's soul.

The remainder of this case study highlights some of the subjects that can evoke real depth of poetic expression with young children and includes a variety of examples and should be viewed therefore as an anthology, not a developmental programme. Children are individuals and can often surprise adults in their expression of views on life and the experiences they undertake. Children who may exhibit difficulty in certain writing forms can suddenly produce a poem using deeply imaginative language when freed from the traditional constraints imposed by many writing tasks. As poems are very personal statements, every poem a child writes should be viewed and valued on individual terms and not compared by the teacher with some hazy ideal.

Of moors, mists and darkened forests

We have found that the best poetry often comes from a first-hand experience. Feelings evoked by actual experiences during school visits can be very personal but a written description of the visit can sometimes end in the production of rather stilted responses. In poetry, the experiences can really come alive. Even so, it is interesting to see how similar experiences can evoke so many different responses. Where some poetry is very descriptive in nature, for example in 'The Wood' by Tracy, aged eight, 'A Tree Poem' by Beverley, aged eight, which was written following the same experience, evokes real mysticism, perhaps sharing an inner fear or nightmare which was obviously worrying her, in a safe, unthreatening way.

The use of literary devices, for example metaphor, alliteration, and personification is made even at this young age, and shows well the influence of poetry reading upon these writers.

A Tree Poem.

This twisty twiny monster
Reaching out with his thousands of
long arms reaching out to catch
me!
Thousands and thousands of them,
diffrent shapes diffrent sizes, reaching
high up to the sky.

This Monster hasnt an eye
And only has one leg,
Crinkled lines all over his body
Green oval things sprouting out
all over,
It has millons of long and
short feet.

This monster hardly moves
We hardly see him att
all
He just sways from side to

Side.
When he's mad he gives a
little rustle so we know he's
very mad. So becareful where
ever you go hell be
THERE!

A Tree Poem by Beverley, aged eight

The wood

The Trees Blowing aBout in the wind
a cod Breeze over Head
The Birds Singing in The Trees
The trout Jumping a bout in The stream
The soft feelings in the air
stop Bequiet I here the wind whspering in my ear
The leaves palling so softly on to the ground
I here the stream making a soft sound rushing Hurrying
a way to a nother part of The stream
The Soft Breeze Blowing all the leaves on the ground
which rock in The air
and lands softly on The ground
not a single noise to Be Heard
When the trout Jumps out of the stream
a round Shape is made
not one But a lot and alot of pratty patterns
The wind gos down our neck
as we walk a long a smell of wild garlic came to ournosi
and The Smell op perfumed plowers rocking in The wind.

The Wood by Tracy, aged eight

The senses play a big part in children's descriptive poetry and here it is interesting to note how the weather can greatly affect children's perceptions of a visit. Compare 'The Wood' by Tracy (above) and 'Bierley Wood' by Nichola (opposite). Both describe the same place but at different times of the year.

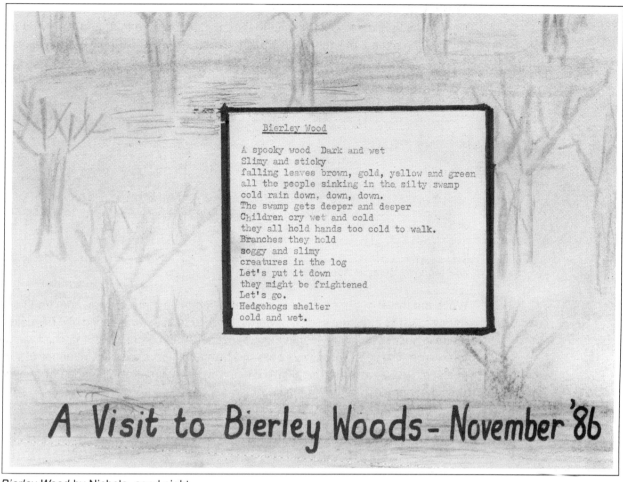

Bierley Wood

A spooky wood Dark and wet
Slimy and sticky
falling leaves brown, gold, yellow and green
all the people sinking in the silty swamp
cold rain down, down, down.
The swamp gets deeper and deeper
Children cry wet and cold
they all hold hands too cold to walk.
Branches they hold
soggy and slimy
creatures in the log
Let's put it down
they might be frightened
Let's go.
Hedgehogs shelter
cold and wet.

A Visit to Bierley Woods - November '86

Bierley Wood by Nichola, aged eight

Poetry can describe an experience using direct, unsophisticated language, for example 'Walking in the Rain' by Kulbir, aged six, but similarly the phrase 'The herd of fuss starts again' in 'Poem' by Nicola, aged six, gives the reader a real picture of what the scene was actually like.

POEM

The shivering water falls
Zooming along.
Bumping up over the deep sharp stones.
Twirling round round
It's quietness now
Then suddenly
The herd of fuss starts again
It's rushing down the steep hill
As quick as it can
I climbed higher and higher
As I pretended to be the river
It's beating now against the rock
For ever more, it slows down.

Poem by Nicola, aged six

WALKING IN THE RAIN

Here comes the water
tumbling down over
the rocks and me as
I scramble up the stream
soggy wet through
with wellies full to
the top with water.

Walking in the Rain by Kulbir, aged six

The night

Many young children have a genuine fear of night and the dark and poetry on this subject can often highlight the depth of these anxieties. Children will often express these anxieties through the literary devices available to them, for example the fear of being watched or followed being interpreted as the moon in the poem 'The Night' by Gemma, aged five.

```
THE NIGHT


The night is dark and gloomy
Every thing is creeping through the night
The moon is watching them till morning light has come
Then all day they are asleep
The owl is as wise as us they say.
```

The Night by Gemma, aged five

While the thrust of our comments on poetry has been a move away from traditional rhyme towards the creative use of words, there are cases when song-like rhyme and metre is successful in developing the messages and moods which the child wishes to express. The poem 'A Snowy Poem' by Zoë, aged nine, shows the influence of song in a positive way and also highlights a different view of poetry influenced by the very personal impressions of the night.

A Snowy Poem

1. It was cold that December night,
   but I was warm,
   we went for a walk in the crispy snow
   it was clear that night when the moon shone bright
   we went for a walk in the snow.

2. we went for a walk
   the snow was crisp and bright
   there in the dusk the hall was standing
   a black silhouette in the night
   it was clear that night when the moon shone bright
   we went for a walk in the snow.

3. The lanterns shone bright
   in the night
   red, green, yellow and blue
   there they were in the night
   shining very, very, very bright
   when we went for a walk in the snow.

A Snowy Poem by Zoë, aged nine

The city

The following two poems present different views of the city. 'The City' by Martin, aged eight, was a culmination of ideas following a project on Dawn and gives his view of what the city would be like as dawn breaks. 'The City Storm' by Mark, aged seven, followed an actual experience during a school visit into Bradford city centre. Once again the use of simile, for example 'like giants', and the creative use of language in 'The City' by Martin are able to convey a true impression and change in tempo as the city comes to life.

```
THE CITY


The big buildings are like giants
Standing like great big Christmas trees.
The sky is all orange
And the sky-scrapers are tall, black silhouettes.
The sky is all different colours
Against the moving monster.
The giant scrapers grow taller and wider every minute.
Crowded shops are open, the lights come on.
Sky-scrapers light up,
One floor by one floor.
Everything is alive.
Newspaper boys calling out,
Cars sounding their horns.
People walking, people talking,
Most of them going home from the night shift.
```

The City by Martin, aged eight

```
THE CITY STORM


The rain comes firing down like spitfires shooting
and the town clock ringing.
The power is too strong.
The one o' clock gun fires.
The water splashing all around and
headlights dazzling,motor bikes whizzing past.

The birds perched up high in the tops of buildings,
looking for some scraps of food and going in markets.
Some clouds,all dull but a little sun in the sky.
The storm turns to hail,like thunder striking you.
The hail turns to snow --- and turns back
and feels like helpless falling tears.
```

The City Storm by Mark, aged seven

We cannot overemphasise the value of the first-hand experience in extending children's writing. Throughout this case study, the deepest, most sensitive poetry has consistently been that written by children having actually experienced feelings or events from first hand. School visits into the country or woodland, when children are transported into different environments and physically immersed within a new atmosphere, are so stimulating to the senses and evoke real pictures. These images remain so clear that their translation into words will draw the most expressive use of language. In the same way as outdoor visits provide these unforgettable images from children, so visits to museums can equally provoke imaginative thought as the child

65

both experiences an atmosphere and an empathy with the past. The value of the 'in house' experience also merits a mention in this section – for example, animals and birds brought into the classroom can stimulate real description in the poetic mode as the following poem shows.

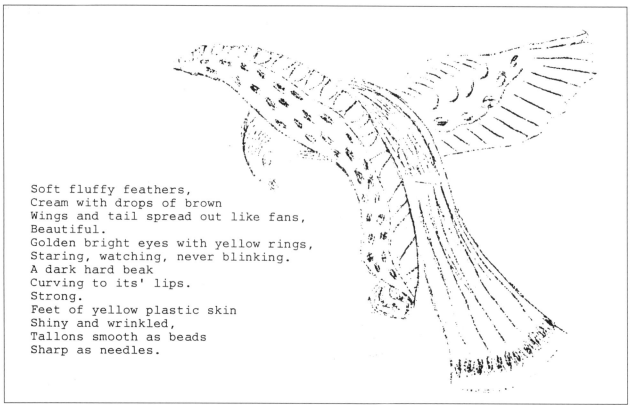

Soft fluffy feathers,
Cream with drops of brown
Wings and tail spread out like fans,
Beautiful.
Golden bright eyes with yellow rings,
Staring, watching, never blinking.
A dark hard beak
Curving to its' lips.
Strong.
Feet of yellow plastic skin
Shiny and wrinkled,
Tallons smooth as beads
Sharp as needles.

Kestrel by Lindsay, aged eight, drawing by Paul, aged eight

Illustrated poetry

The actual illustration of poetry can often shape the language and form of a poem itself. This becomes an integral part of the poem for many children. Illustrations often give the poem shape and character and should be encouraged wherever possible. The examples on pp.67-8 are included to emphasise the importance of illustration as part of the whole creative process of the writing of poetry.

On a thoughtful note

It would not be right to end this short anthology without mention of the very deep, thoughtful poetry young children can produce when an experience or issue has either specific relevance or has captured their genuine concern. Jeffcoate's (1979) vision of schools providing an open forum for the discussion of emotive issues, such as attitudes to disability, racism, cruelty etc., is a positive step towards children developing the skills and understanding required to challenge the prejudices and stereotyped images presented by society. Such issues and concerns can often generate real sensitivity from young children and therefore opportunities for the discussion and expression of these feelings should form an essential part of the school ethos. The examples on p.69 show the beginnings of signs of empathy and questioning, so important if children are to be encouraged to make their own choices and decisions and fashion their own values and preferences based upon personal knowledge and not society's influence.

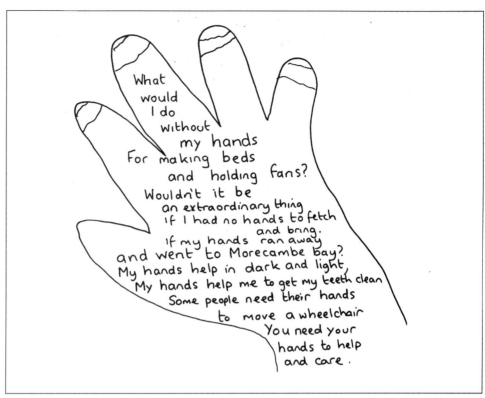

What
would
I do
without
my hands
For making beds
and holding fans?
Wouldn't it be
an extraordinary thing
If I had no hands to fetch
and bring.
If my hands ran away
and went to Morecambe Bay?
My hands help in dark and light,
My hands help me to get my teeth clean
Some people need their hands
to move a wheelchair
You need your
hands to help
and care.

Hands by Caroline, aged six

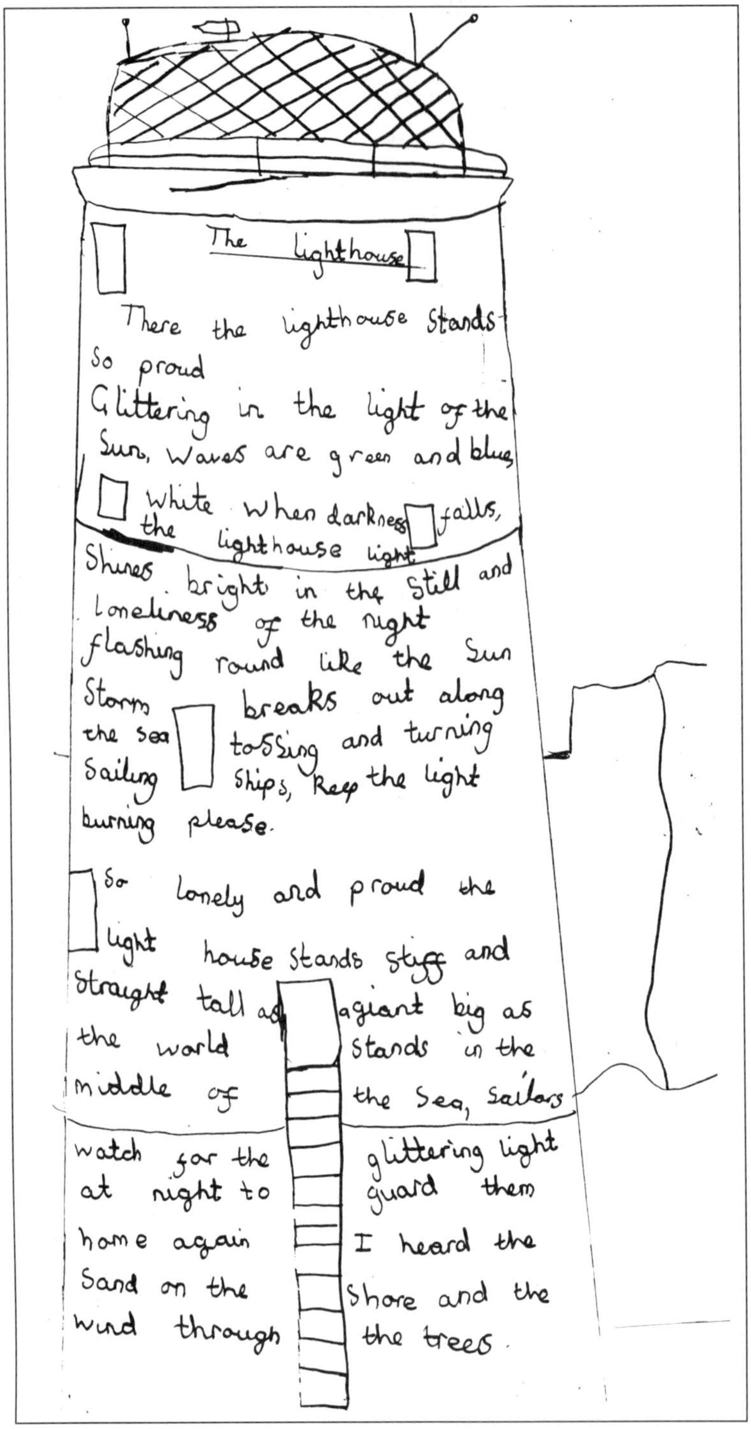
The lighthouse
There the lighthouse stands
So proud
Glittering in the light of the
Sun, Waves are green and blue
white when darkness falls,
the lighthouse light
Shines bright in the still and
Loneliness of the night
flashing round like the Sun
Storm breaks out along
the sea tossing and turning
Sailing ships, Keep the light
burning please.
So lonely and proud the
light house stands stiff and
Straight tall as agiant big as
the world stands in the
middle of the Sea, Sailors
watch for the glittering light
at night to guard them
home again I heard the
Sand on the Shore and the
wind through the trees.

The Lighthouse by Beverley, aged eight

verse 1. Captured, Yet Wanting To Be Free.

Flying about,
Fluttering Wings,
Over the Sea,
Goes Me,
Big and beautiful I go about,
But. Help!
I have been captured,
In a net,
Help!. I cry again,
As I am pinned onto the wall,
Goodbye! My friends,
Goodbye!.

Captured Yet Wanting To Be Free by Claire, aged eight

```
                              WHALES

In the old days we needed to kill whales because we needed to have margarine,
perfume and soap and meat and fat and corsets and hard combs and necklaces
and other things.  But that was for the old days.  But why now when we've
got all of those things.  We don't need to kill whales any more.  Why should
we kill whales it is cruel and unkind, it's like us being stabbed and stabbed
until you die.  I bet you wouldn't like to be killed, whales do not kill us
so we're in no harm because if we still kill whales the whales will start
being our enemies and then we'd be in danger.  The whales are mammals and
they are hardly any different to us.  Whales have got thousands of centuries
to go yet and they are nearly extinct so try not to kill any more whales
they are nearly extinct and if you want a world to be a world please don't
ruin the world.  For if you do you'll be punished for it by God.  But we do
not need whales any more.  So why should we hunt them.
```

Whales by Vicky, aged seven

Case study: Developing story

A story is an expression of feelings about life (Parker 1969). The reader of a story perceives and contemplates these feelings which are formulated and mediated through the elements of story. The author establishes the rules and seeks to gain our attention by constructing interesting situations which arouse our expectations. The beginnings of stories are of paramount importance since they set the scene from which the action will emanate. A second feature of a story as a form is our anticipation of a climax followed by the sense of an ending which, if the story is to prove successful, must fit happily with its opening and middle.

Stories contain universal characteristics and feelings which children include in the stories they make for themselves. Telling stories about animals, toys and machines is a widespread phenomenon. Animals represent biological beings which allow us

<u>Nicole and the Giant Cake.</u>

I was in bed when my Mother shouted up the stairs "There's a letter for you Nicole with 'INPORTANT' stamped all over it." "Alright I'm coming its probably another order" I said (My Mother is called Kathy I am sixteen years old I'm a baker it is the year 1971). I came sliding down the bannister and jumped onto the Hall floor. Kathy gave me the letter I opened it and inside this is what it said

Buckingham Palace

Dear Nicole
                I am having a party at the palace and I am going to have a big feast but unfortunately my Cheif Cook has resigned so will you please come and fill in the space. I need a big giant cake baking, a cake big enough to feed nine hundred and and seventy eight hungry people. I have four maids, four cooks, two waiters and two butlers, all waiting to be told what to do. Will you please write an answer back. If you want to come, come on the first of January at four o'clock in the afternoon.
                Your's Sincerley
                the Queen.

"Mother, it's a letter from the Queen asking me whether I want to be Cheif Cook at the palace, can I" I said "Of course you can if you want to" said Mother "Write an answer straight away" so I went upstairs and wrote an answer. This is what I put

58 Shay Drive
London

Dear Queen
                I would be delighted to come to the palace and be Cheif Cook. I will be there at four o'clock o'clock on January the first
                Yours Sincerley
                Nicole Bradley.

Nicole and the Giant Cake by Celia, aged nine

to channel emotions towards them. It is possible and even necessary to love, hate, admire and even fear creatures depicted in story. Stories contain universal feelings, for example a need for security, a need for affection, a need to play with fear and so on. Children recognise such feelings and include them in their work. The presence of dolls and toys in stories which children make up or read is of psychological importance. These characters usually depend on the child and are not his or her equal. It forms a sort of role-reversal to that of the child and adult because here the child is superior to the toy. They are common features in children's storywriting and explain further 'what they are up to' when they write.

I was really pleased that I had been asked but there was one snag if the cake was going to be a big cake it would need a big oven, and big mixers everything would have to be bought, unless the Queen had some very big mixers and ovens.

So I told my Dad and he said "I don't know of any big giant mixers and ovens but I will look around". Then there was a knock at the door "rater–tat-tat" I opened it, it was Joanne Randel asking me If I was playing I said "Yes, why don't we go and play in the woods" So we did. When we got there I told Joanne about my offer from the Queen. Joanne said "Why don't you make your own oven and mixer" "What a good idea, we will try that" I said. Then Joanne went home for her dinner.

The next day I packed my clothes it was December the thirty first my last day at home.

On January the first I caught a red bus at seven o'clock a.m it smelt of cigarettes, but it wasn't so bad. When I got to the palace I had to persuade the guards to let me through the gate. I was just wondering where to go, when the Queen came along a corridor and said "I will show you around the palace, follow me." Then with a swish of her robes she walked briskly towards the kitchen. We went through lots and lots of passages and corridors covered with tapestries and paintings till at last we came to the kitchen. The Queen showed me around and said "A hem stand in your order please," then she turned to me and said "The first four girls are the maids, the next are the cooks, then the waiters and last but not least the two butlers." "Now then I will say their names in the order that they are standing in, Kate, Joey, Julie, Rachel   Nicola, Ruth, Julia, Vicky   Timothy, John Robert, Peter everyone this is Nicole she is your new Chief Cook" Then the Queen left me to myself. I said "Well then lets start finding the ingredients for the giant cake" So I, Rachel, and Ruth put the ingredients in a big bowl while Kate, Joey and Julie got the ingredients for us. We put in the big bowl ten bags of flour

seven eggs
six packets of raisens
one tin of coce powder
three packets of butter
four pounds of salt?
and ten drops of peppermint.

Nicole and the Giant Cake cont.

71

When I and Rachel and Ruth had put all that in we looked around for a big mixer but there wasn't one. So I sent Peter up to ask the Queen if there were any big mixers in the palace. He came down with the answer "The Queen will be coming down shortly" that was a reilef the Queen would be able to do something about it. The Queen came down a minute later I said "Have you got any big giant mixers for us to use dear Queen" "Yes, as a matter of fact we have I ordered them a week ago for the giant cake. Timothy, John, Peter and Robert will you come and get them, follow me". We waited and waited till Timothy, John, Peter and Robert came panting through the kitchen door door carrying two giant mixers and one giant oven. We put the mixer mixers in a corner corner of the room and then we got back to work. The mixture was put in the mixer and then Nicola switched it on, there was a big whirring whirring sound as the mixer turned round and round faster and faster then suddenly "Crash"!! one mixer broke into little bits and the cake mixture flew everywhere. Kate, Joey, Julie and Rachel all said "Oh" Nicola, Ruth, Julia and Vicky all said "Eee" and Timothy, Robert, Peter, John and I just stood there in amazement We slowly stooped down and picked up all the mixture which had flown out of the mixer (when it broke) and put it in the other one. Then I said "Julie and Ruth will you please remove all of whats left of the mixer." When everything was back to normal again we normal, we started all over again. Whirr went the mixer round and round it went.

Then Kate said "When do we stop it" in a very loud voice. "About now" I answered back. So we stopped the mixer and then put the mixture for the giant cake in a giant cake tin. Then Robert and John put the cake in the giant oven, Julie turned the oven to number five on the oven and the giant cake started to cook. When the giant cake was cooked Joey and Vicky made the white icing and they put it on. Joey and Vicky had to stand on a very high chair to get to reach the top of the cake. I said "Kate and Rachel will you please go and tell the Queen that the giant cake is iced and made" So we waited and waited till Kate and Rachel came through the kitchen door with the Queen. The Queen Queen said "We will have to get the cake through the door somehow", "But how are we going to do it" said Julie "By pushing heaving pulling and trying hard" said the Queen. So we got the giant cake on its side and Kate, Joey, Julia, the Queen, Vicky, Rachel and I went round the other side of the door and Julie, Ruth, Nicola, Peter, John, Timothy and Robert

Nicole and the Giant Cake cont.

pushed and pushed then suddenly! the cake went right through the door.
"We're through, we're through" shouted Julie.
That afternoon everything was set out on a table, ~~When~~ (It was the party
that the giant cake was for) When the guests had all sat down the Lord
Mayoress said "Ladies, Gentelmen, Boys and Girls I am now going to cut this giant
cake oh dear I can't reach the top of the cake will somebody please fetch
me a high chair to stand on (so the Lord Mayor brought a high chair for
the Lord Mayoress to stand on) I will now proudly cut this magnificent giant
cake" Then when the Lord Mayoress stood on tiptoes to cut the cake SPLAT!!.
she fell into the giant cake icing, Everyone gave a cry of horror the Queen
said "Come with me Lady Mayoress, we will see what we can do for you". Then the Lord
Mayor cut the cake safely and everyone had a piece (a big one too).
Then the children played games and the adults danced. After all the guests had
gone the Queen came to me and said "Thankyou so much, please will you make
another giant cake the people liked it so much."
    So it started all over again.

Nicole and the Giant Cake cont.

Stories have an educative value in the presentation of kinds of situations children need to cope with daily. It is comforting for children to discover that others have emotions similar to their own. If, however, a child produces a story of his own which we feel is outside these boundaries, then we should examine it very closely – the child may be trying to tell us something very profound and significant.

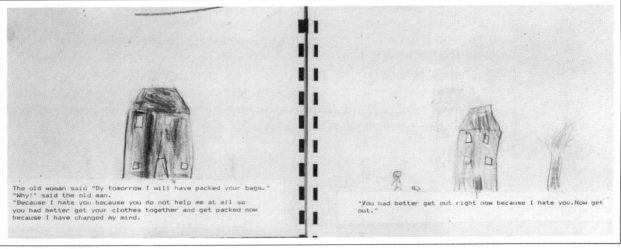

Bound and illustrated story by Darren, aged seven.

Nancy Martin (1976) tells how reshaping an experience in talking or writing has the power:

to transmute events or feelings that were painful or disquieting when they were experienced directly into a new experience.

Autobiographical narrative is a necessary part of human understanding. We have to tell about our personal experience in order to understand it. It is not always desirable or possible to write these experiences directly into story, so magic is often used. Magic can help us resolve our problems and this device can be seen in children's storywriting, partly because of their experience of stories which employ magic and myth, but also because as yet they have not reached a level of thinking which enables them to handle fully 'cause and effect' in narrative. Magical events enable the author to deal with indescribable or inexplicable events. They provide an easy solution to the situations children write themselves into.

The act of creating stories has been likened to embarking upon a voyage of discovery with little idea of destination. Burgess (1977) tells us that children draw upon their primary and secondary experience and organise it through words to produce a story or a 'construct'. Stories can either be about something which actually happened or something the author invented. The key point for teachers is to concern themselves with the quality of what goes on inside the child's head, a view endorsed by the Bullock Report (DES/WO 1975, p.8):

What is the quality of the child's verbalisation of his experience? With what fidelity and coherence does he communicate it to his readers?

From our experience of sharing stories with young children, we believe it is possible to identify characteristics which seem to permeate storywriting and seem to illustrate children's ability to select and shape language in order to bring the experience to life. Children present direct pictures of childhood, often presenting sensitivity to the range of characters' feelings. They display their own strength of character and often demonstrate reasoning power. Some stories portray childhood dreams, authors writing themselves into situations which offer opportunities to play the hero, test the security they already have and sometimes play with fear.

A universal and therapeutic feeling that children often use in their storywriting is that of humour. Humour is an affective reaction and the development of humour follows a general pattern. This pattern is said to parallel and be dependent upon the child's intellectual and emotional development. According to Kappas (1967), a nine-year-old's sense of humour is much finer in form and content than that of the five-year-old. The humour of nine-year-olds may also reveal some hostility and aggression and they enjoy situations which deviate from the norm. They often enjoy telling jokes and riddles and often include them in their stories.

Children, it seems, enjoy testing the security they already have. The significance of a journey or quest in story is to find something out about ourselves.

No one undertakes an arduous journey without learning about himself and discovering something to do with his identity.

(Lavender 1977)

Often this journey releases children from what is everyday and ordinary into a world that involves deeper feelings. As Peel (1967) explains,

Children's fantasy changes markedly as they go up the Junior School. The secure domesticity goes. Fears predominate, personal hopes and ambitions are acted out.

Some children, however, need security and nowhere is this need better demonstrated than in the endings children write. The happy ending can be viewed as a consolation for most children. However, when we are confronted with a story which does not obey this characteristic and provides a problematic ending, then we must stop and consider why.

The skill of a good storyteller is to make the reader feel comfortable in the story world. Often we can be disappointed when stories children write begin well but are not sustained. One technique which works well is modelling. Children are given a diagram with clues as to elements that need to be included in the story. In the example on pp. 76-7, Simon, aged eight, was given a drawing of an underground tunnel full of passages, dead-ends and escape routes finally reaching the sea. This enabled him to produce his story. The ideas were all his, but the 'model' gave a structure to the story and the reader feels extremely comfortable with it.

The more children write stories, the more they learn about storywriting. They come to realise the emotional and imaginative outlet of storywriting and are capable of producing enjoyable and satisfying stories. In many stories it is possible to detect a sense of 'felt life', or to identify divergent thinkers, or perhaps to feel the child's personality screaming out at you as you read their offerings. Certainly, the power of fiction and the influence of storywriting upon the development of a child's writing style must not be underestimated. It is perhaps the first print form young children are formally introduced to and, as such, may remain a powerful influence throughout a writer's life.

Adventure at the wedding

The photographs at the wedding were taking place. Winston noticed a scrap of paper on a gravestone. He picked it up. He looked at it. It was a treasure map! There was some writing on it which said "move the grave stone". When no-one was looking he pushed against the stone. It moved easily. There were some steps leading down. Winston wasn't dressed for caving in his top-hat and tails. But he wanted to be rich. He started down. The steps were green with slime. Winston thought he would slip. Suddenly the stairs ended. In front of him were some coal black boulders. Above him were bright yellow stalagtites. Winston wondered if he could crawl between the boulders and the stalagtites. He tried it. The stalagtites were inches away from his back. He made it through that problem but another one blocked his path. In front of him was a pit full of water about 10 metres deep and 3 metres wide. Winston decided to jump it. He took a run up and leapt over the pit. He walked on a bit until he came to a gap in the floor of the cave with a rope hanging over it. He didn't drop down the gap because he could kill himself. He grabbed the rope and swung across. Winston started to walk. But he felt tierd and hungry. He was so tierd that he didn't notice some gaps in the floor. He fell down one and landed with a bump and fell unconscious. He came round an hour later. By this time people were getting worried. Winston found a key and some food. He rested

Adventure at the Wedding by Simon, aged eight

and regained his strength. He put the key in his pocket and forgot about it. He climbed out and found a rope in front of him he climbed down and saw a ladder. He climbed down it and slid down a moss covered slide. In front of him was a door marked treasure room. The door was locked. Winston remembered the key. He put it in the key hole and turned it. The door swung open! Inside Winston saw a treasure chest that was open. In it were Diamonds, Fire opals, Emeralds, Rubys, Jewels of all kinds. Winston ran forward. But the door and the chest slamed shut. Winston tried the doors. They didnt open. He tried to put the key in the locks. One opened. I front of him was a ladder. Winston went down 3 ladders. He ran forward, through an entrance and fell into the sea. He stood up. He saw a entrance. He went into it. There were some steps leading up. He went up. Winston came out on the cliff near the church. His mum and dad saw him. They said "Winston you silly boy why did you come up here. People were worried about you." Winston smiled. They never new the true story.

Adventure at the Wedding cont.

6 The Expressive Aims of Writing

So much of children's writing is based upon their life experiences that we must acknowledge that what they read or write will not only involve their thoughts but also their feelings. We understand the word 'feeling' to refer to the process of shaping and ordering the intuitive, imaginative, and emotional explorations of the mind. Much research has been done in the area of thinking and intelligence, but the area of feelings and emotions in children's writing is still to be fully explored. What is known is that the emotions play a very important part in our lives. Moods change, joy and laughter can soon turn to sadness and despair and these emotional states can greatly affect relationships, colour judgements and affect the decisions we make. Traditionally, the expression of emotions in public has therefore been viewed as a weakness of character, an indication of instability or insecurity. Emotions, however, are not the weaknesses of character structure that people would have us believe. We all have emotions and feelings and it is only through the exhibiting of these that we develop as individual characters with individual principles, concerns and attitudes. It is often difficult for young children to express their inner feelings and emotions openly, inhibited by societal and peer pressure. Children should be given both the encouragement and the opportunities to express such emotions and feelings in a safe and receptive environment, however, as it is a natural step towards the development of a child's whole personality.

Expressive writing helps children to release many of these inhibitions and gives them a safe avenue for the expression of personal feelings and emotions. Writing can be a very private activity where children have the freedom to express themselves in the knowledge that their written thoughts will be secret and will not receive a wider audience, but at the same time gives them opportunities to release the tensions and personal emotions from within. It allows a way of simply 'letting off steam' without causing the child distress of the kind often experienced when relating troubles and emotional experiences orally to another person. The knowledge that such writing is secret and 'for their eyes only' can often help children to regard it as a safe way of telling the truth without the worry of being judged or the information being used to further add to their emotional problems.

It is important that children are given opportunities for private thought and writing but the term 'expressive writing' covers much more than this. It is an opportunity for the individual to assert him or herself and his or her own views and feelings on issues that s/he regards as being of great personal importance. Children have views that are equally important to those of the teacher and society at large and therefore opportunities for the expression of these views need to be made. In writing, their expression with young children requires not only the structuring of thought, logic and delivery but requires support in the same way dialogue support is given by a conversational partner. To ignore and not support such an avenue of expression could be depriving young children of the foundations needed to build individual confidence, self-esteem and personal worth and value. The making of protest and the assertion of personal beliefs and values is a form of writing that is often regarded as beyond the capabilities of young children. The argument against this, however, must be that when an issue has immediate relevance or is of particular interest to a child, then s/he will produce views orally that far outweigh those of adults to whom the issue may not have the same relevance or immediacy. If sufficient support is given to the child in the form of encouragement and perhaps advice, within an overall atmosphere of trust and mutual respect, so much a part of creative teacher–pupil relationship, then the structuring of logic and compiling of protests in text form does not seem to be the very large step it first appeared. Young children do rely heavily upon the support of a conversational partner when ordering their logic and ideas. Therefore, without the support of a creative teacher–pupil relationship and this atmosphere of trust and respect, the situation can arise where a child has made an active contribution in discussion, sharing views and putting forward opinions with clarity, but when asked to continue this into writing, s/he seems unable to make a start.

Despite the importance of this form of expressive protest, however, expressive discourse with young children is traditionally seen at a more subjective, personal level. This may be, for example, the writing of memories of a relative or favourite pet recently deceased, the writing of personal impressions and reflections following a visit perhaps to a dark dungeon, or being open in describing people and their own relationships with them.

In order to give children the opportunities to develop the confidence of expression beyond this 'personal experience' level, it is important that expressive writing is viewed by the teacher in its widest terms, incorporating opportunities for the very private form of expression; the expression of feelings surrounding the personal or shared experience with a trusted audience; and also the deeper emotions of anger or guilt in the form of expressive protest. Only through the provision of all three, within an environment of trust, acceptance and mutual respect, can real freedom of expression develop.

As teachers, we should strive to give children the confidence to express their personal beliefs and feelings over a variety of real issues and concerns. Belief-orientated and fierce argument can often lead to the expression of real sincerity and the writing of deeply emotional statements. Protests and anger over wider issues, for example pollution, vandalism, name-calling and the treatment of animals can all provoke very deep reactions among children, reactions and emotions that are an inevitable part of daily life and should not be ignored. The provision of opportunities for discussion at this level, with the encouragement of both expressive argument and critical consciousness among children, is central to a multicultural/antiracist approach to education where children question attitudes and injustices and contribute to societal change. Therefore, to provide opportunities for such writing will give children not only the expression of self-awareness and empathy with others but will build their sense of relationship with the wider world and the world issues that affect us all. Such views are value-laden and greatly influenced by the media, the children's peers and society in general but, if sensitively introduced and discussed openly in a non-threatening environment (the teacher providing the balanced view when required), then young children are quite capable of mature expression, reasoned argument and determined protest. The need to extend this form of expressive discourse must not be underestimated.

It is difficult to advise people how to develop expressive writing with young children. Certainly there is no magical key or stimulus that once given to children will lead to the unleashing of personal feeling and emotion. The work of Witkin (1974) provides some interesting and useful thoughts which are particularly applicable when thinking about expression in children's storywriting. His main argument is that the teacher's role is vital – the pupil will need help in resolving his feelings through a realised form. His plea is that teachers recognise the need for subjective expression and that they should not be afraid to acknowledge the 'live wire' of the power of emotion. Teachers need to be supportive and tactful in offering guidance but should not control the medium of language too tightly. Therefore what the teacher must do is support interests or issues identified as being important by the children themselves and, through the provision of stimuli, experiences and the materials to support and extend these issues, the teacher must be able to both support and balance the views and opinions being exchanged. Jeffcoate (1979) goes further and emphasises the need for teachers discussing racism with children to support and be sympathetic towards white racist children as well as the antiracists. While appreciating that Jeffcoate's comments were aimed at the teaching of older children, the underlying message is the same for younger pupils. When young children are deeply involved in an issue and have very strong opinions, it would be wrong for the teacher to dominate the discussion and force his or her own views upon the children, even if done in an implicit rather than explicit way. The teacher should purely provide the balanced view if required, encouraging the development of the skills to question, discuss and then make decisions when required.

Children need the encouragement to release their emotions and talk openly on a variety of subjects, sharing unpleasant as well as pleasant experiences in a caring classroom environment built around mutual respect for each other and for each other's views and beliefs. This can only lead to children feeling at ease with those around them and being freed from the normal inhibitions a less caring environment would create. Children need to know that if they say or write exactly what they feel, their discourse will be accepted seriously and not ridiculed or demeaned by others.

The following projects highlight examples of stimuli and issues that captured the imagination of young children, encouraging expressive writing and protest among six- to nine-year-old children. The projects themselves developed in classrooms where an open forum for discussion had been established and where children were encouraged to talk openly and share ideas and feelings in the knowledge that their spoken and written thoughts would be respected and valued by all. Times for the group discussion of emotive issues were regularly incorporated into the structure of the classroom whenever and wherever the need arose.

Case study: Bradford – a beautiful place?

As part of an environmental awareness programme with a class group of seven- to eight-year-old children, a project was negotiated with the National Museum of Photography in Bradford. The aim of the project was to introduce the children to the workings of polaroid and thirty-five millimetre cameras and to give the children greater control over decision-making and the development and direction the project was to take. Ultimately, the children were to be given control of their own learning experiences. As the children were going to use both colour and monochrome film, it was anticipated that the photographs would be compared and contrasted, the children developing a greater understanding of the strengths and weaknesses each medium possesses and ultimately being able to identify when colour or monochrome would be the most suitable according to which image the child wanted to present.

The subject of the photographs was not to be an autocratic decision taken by the teacher but was to be a consensus, a group decision taken by the children themselves. As a great deal of work had centred around Bradford and environmental care, however, it was not surprising that children initially chose to look at the city centre and record positive attempts that had been made to improve the environment there. The children were given the freedom and the time to look at the city centre and choose specific 'shots' themselves that highlighted its pleasant side, images that the Bradford tourist industry would like to foster. The children took this responsibility and although a few children took photographs on impulse, most deliberated over which subject material was to be included and spent time ensuring that the 'shot' was exactly as they wanted. The children in small groups were encouraged to make written notes at the time of taking the photograph, including the time, position and reason for taking it. These would then help as reminders when the children returned to school. These photographs and notes were then taken and compared with each other back at school. Discussion focused upon the reasons why such images would attract tourism to Bradford.

In discussion, it became clear that the children knew themselves what they wanted to portray. They had strong ideas about what would constitute a pleasant and attractive image of the city, but were perhaps less certain as to the reasons why. This firm belief, but difficulty in explaining its logic, was surely an indication of the way in which children's judgements and preferences are influenced from a very early age by society and the values it holds. Even very young children are subsumed by this influence and are conditioned in their understanding of right and wrong, good and bad, etc. With the polaroid photographs, the children knew that flowers, grass and 'tasteful' statues presented a positive image but could not explain why. This inert belief, conditioned by societal values and reaffirmed constantly by media images, proved to be very strong.

The teacher wanted the children to probe below the surface and develop a greater understanding and confidence in explaining why the images presented what they did. Although the intention was never to counter society's influence upon the children's attitudes, it was the intention to encourage the children to use the images they had photographed and develop their confidence by sharing their unbiased, personal feelings regarding Bradford as it really was.

All the blossom on the trees
near the fountain make the
area look attractive and
there is not a lot of rubbish.
There is a lamp post behind a
tree with blossom on it. It is
a beautiful picture with no
people. It has no fish and chip
papers.

Writing about Bradford by Michael, aged seven

Searching out the truth

The positive aspects of the city centre were discussed further and the obverse was introduced. If these images highlighted the positive side of Bradford city centre, what images would show the negative side of things? Great discussion centred around the problems that had received a high profile in the local press. Vandalism, litter, industrial decline and racial tension had all been featured in the local press and had done much to highlight the negative side of Bradford. The children had very definite ideas of specific buildings and environments that would portray this negative image and were able to approach the second photographic experience with a clearly defined purpose and understanding.

Once the general subject matter had been discussed, a decision had to be taken about whether to use colour or monochrome film. Black and white photographs were contrasted with colour and children discussed which medium would better portray the image they wanted. They chose monochrome as it not only contrasted with the 'brighter' colour pictures already taken but would also add to the feeling of darkness and depression.

The children returned to the city centre and, using thirty-five millimetre cameras with monochrome film, began to search for images that contrasted the positive face of Bradford already captured on film. Graffiti, litter, vandalism and dereliction were all carefully captured on film. The results were clear, depressing images of a city centre in decline. The children looked through the images, discussed them and began to write about them and express their personal feelings.

THE OLD BUILDING

Smashed windows boarded up
Broken pipes along the wall.
Crumbling bricks, old and
dark.
Crane all rusty and old
doors,
All dark and spooky.

For the people who work
there, I don't think its
spooky.
They're used to it and they
like the place.
They do not like all the
graffiti at the bottom of
the doors,
and smashed bottles,
and crisp packets,
and sweet wrappers on the
floor.

The Old Building and photograph by Mark, aged seven

Although the teacher did not want to interfere and lead the children's thoughts and ideas, she did want to encourage real depth of feeling and expression in the children's writing. Therefore, rather than standing on the periphery of things, leaving the children in total isolation, she encouraged them to share their work in progress and decided to talk with them in group conferences of the kind highlighted in Chapter Three. The children became involved in making suggestions to each other, posing questions for further thought and extending the creative pupil–pupil and pupil–teacher relationship already established.

The partner-support system encouraged children to give greater thought and ultimately greater depth to their writing. Where a child knew what s/he wanted to say but lacked confidence and constantly sought teacher approval for his or her work, the partner-support system encouraged the development of self-confidence and the following of his or her own instincts. The resultant writing expressed real maturity and an imaginative use of vocabulary.

> POISONOUS PRISON
>
> Water rushing down below
> and under the bridge,
> on it goes,
> rippling on stones as it
> goes by.
> Poisonous water because
> of vandals throwing bricks
> in,
> splash they go!
> Water rushing by an old
> house,
> windows are blocked up
> because of vandals, they
> can't get in and smash things
> up.
> If someone fell in there,
> they would never get out.
>
> It would be like a prison.
> Factories in the background,
> signs in the front ground,
> house in the middle.
> Factories closed down,
> slates smashed, tiles
> smashed.
> Signs saying ,
> "CONTAMINATED WATER"
> I feel I would not like to go
> to Bradford.

Poisonous Prison by Richard, aged seven

The actual experience and clearly defined nature of the work gave children the opportunity to control the images they themselves wanted to portray. Involving them in this way – experiencing and deciding upon the images first hand and then using the reproductions of those images to stimulate talk and writing – gave rise to the kind of written detail and imaginative use of language that could never have been expected had the children been presented with a set of photographs in the classroom which had been taken by a third party.

The group conferencing and sharing work in progress with others proved to be an important part of the writing process. The children were able to discuss their work, not as completed pieces for criticism, but as pieces of work in progress, and the writer was able to share his or her thoughts so far and also his or her plans for further development.

This gave the children the opportunity to question and seek both advice and criticism in a way that was neither threatening or negative. It allowed for children to offer suggestions and share their own ideas, stimulating further thought on issues which were very close to their heart.

Case study: Towards a hostel for women

Homes and buildings: a whole school approach
As part of a school's overall experiential learning programme, it had been decided that the whole school would work around the theme of homes and buildings as a way of both widening the children's experience of the variety of building structures and materials in the immediate environment of the school and raising their awareness of the diversity of culture and life in the city of Bradford. It was also seen as a way of opening up the attitudes of children who lived in a very close community in the heart of a large council estate on the edge of the city.

One year group decided to look at houses and homes in the immediate environment and move outwards comparing their position with homes and houses in other parts of the city. Links were made with schools in the Manningham district of Bradford, an inner-city area with closely knit Muslim and Hindu communities. Comparisons were made with the model village of Saltaire and the three communities were then compared with homes and houses in the city centre. Visits were arranged into Bradford city centre, including a visit to a major hotel and also a hostel for homeless men as a way of highlighting different facets of the term 'home' and what this meant to different people.

Concern for the homeless
As one class prepared for their visit to the city centre, it soon became obvious that there was apprehension among many children regarding the visit to the Salvation Army Hostel. In open discussions which were encouraged by the teacher, society and perhaps more personal influences had already coloured the judgements of many children. They knew what they were going to find. Their view of homeless people was a narrow, distorted image based on many negative assumptions regarding both lifestyle and habit.

A long-term discussion on the wrongs of name-calling had been taking place over many months and had established an open forum for the expression of feelings over a number of issues. Therefore, discussion about the actual term of 'tramp' and its many connotations was a natural development, with children expressing their personal views and listening to those of their peers. Some children did not hold with the negative views held by other children in the class and several of them took the discussion further, writing personal statements regarding the homeless.

The Tramp.

The old tired-out thin tramp walked slowly clumsily along the dusty dirty country lane, looking sorrowfully sorrowly at the ground. His face looked as though it had been through a bush backwards, it was very dirty and crinkled. His hair was a chestnut-brown colour, ragged and long. On his cheek was a small deep scar. His eyes were a deep sea-blue. His mouth had a small cut on the lip.

His pale small hands were all crinkled up with old age. His nails were roughly cut and broken.

He was wearing a ragged blue jumper and black trousers which only came down to his ankles. His shoes were brown. He was wearing a white patched coat which didn't look as though it would give any warmth to anyone. His socks were grey and short. He had some food (cheese and bread) wrapped up in some red spotted cloth which was fastened onto a stick. He slung the bundle over his weak shoulder.

The Tramp by Celia, aged eight

> # Why should it Be Left to us to do something
>
> it Should be Left to us. Because we care more about them and we have some money. Nobody care's Because they think they smell But we Know better and they dont Smell. people call them tramps. But it is not fair on them it is not if we call them tramps And we would not Like to Be Called tramps they are homeLas people Because Know one cares about them. and they have no money or food. Why are the people with out any homes Because there wife's have Kicked them out Some of there wife's do not care about them and people force them to go and then they can not find a home

Why Should It Be Left to Us to Do Something? by Zoë, aged seven

During these discussions and the sharing of this written work several children did moderate their views and, by the time of the visit, all the children were, if only on the surface, willing to meet and spend time with the people in the hostel without prejudging them.

The visit

The children, accompanied by teachers and parent helpers, arrived at the Salvation Army Hostel shortly after lunchtime and were given a guided tour of the hostel by a

Salvation Army officer and an introduction to the Salvation Army particularly regarding its work with the homeless. The children were captivated. The hostel was clean, light and airy. It had a dining room, television room and games room with snooker table. Indeed the hostel did not bear any resemblance to the stereotyped image the children were expecting to find.

Questions were asked by the children continually. Where does the food come from? Why are men homeless? How much would it cost to build a hostel? The children listened intently to the officer's replies. Homeless people in the hostel were not 'layabouts' but many included old people whose families could no longer care for them, people evicted from their homes and people who, due to a combination of circumstances, had found themselves in poverty. It was obvious that the stereotyped images discussed prior to the visit were far from the truth. The children were given the opportunity to talk and play cards and dominoes with some of the men in the hostel and relationships between children and adults became warm.

Homeless women – identifying a lack of provision

Back at school, there seemed to be one statement made by the Salvation Army officer that everybody remembered, some showing great concern. There was apparently no hostel for homeless women in Bradford and recent cases were highlighted where some women had been directed to hostels up to eighty miles away. An open forum was again established to allow the group to discuss this point. Sincere statements and deeply-felt opinions were expressed by children and balanced points of view were put by the teacher as possible answers to their questions.

Children were angry. They were discussing deep moral issues connected with gender and equality. They were expressing deeply-felt opinions emotionally, but with conviction and well-reasoned argument. What could they do? It seemed inevitable that they would do something and the children began to write letters of protest, pleas for help and suggest solutions to the immediate problem.

The children mounted a major campaign, saving money to help the Salvation Army and equally putting pressure upon the council for help. Replies to the children's letters were received and viewed on their individual merits: if children were still unhappy with the reply they had received, then a second letter would be sent (p.89).

All children in the class became involved and wrote at their own level, many using Breakthrough Sentence Makers and supporting each other. The issue had raised many concerns and had drawn all the children together, working towards a common purpose. The outline of a play was devised by a group of children and others collaborated in the improvisation of dialogue and argument as they clearly put their case to two children acting as council officers. Dialogue, often heated and assertive, was real and children believed firmly in the cause in which they had become deeply involved.

Protest songs were written and the campaign shared with the whole school. Visits were made to school by local councillors and the matter was taken to the council and given serious consideration.

Courage, conviction and persistance

Not only had the project helped to counter prejudiced views on the homeless, gleaned from society, media and family influence, but it had also allowed the children to question the inequalities in society and do something positive to redress the balance.

dear Queen. we are writing

back to you because we are
Saving up our money for the
Salvation army for a ladies
hostel. in the queens letter
she put it is none of her
business. we are saving up
and we think it is up to
everybody to help.
Love FROM Amanda and
Nicola

Pressure letter from Amanda and Nicola, aged seven

The issue of provision for homeless women had evoked deep questioning and real concern among children and indeed could have been left at that. Through encouragement, the children were able to follow their own feelings and convictions, supporting their views through reasoned argument, and they were able to take on the issue and do something positive to help. The children's protest became real and gave rise not only to emotional statements, but to the expression of firmly-held beliefs and opinions, well-reasoned logic and deep concern. Children had a genuine reason to write. Letters were well constructed and arguments clear. The writing was deeply emotional and expressive, clearly drawing upon the children's innermost feelings.

Case study: Ingleborough Hall – a residential visit

Learning does not always have to take place in the confines of the four walls of a classroom. Residential experiences can offer enormous potential for language activities both during the children's stay or at a later time back in school. The following examples are a collection of work gathered over the past ten years as a result of visits to Ingleborough Hall, Clapham, in the Yorkshire Dales. Some of the writing reflects the excitement and sense of achievement felt by the children, whilst other pieces portray the emotional aspects such experiences can evoke.

The children could take part in a variety of caving experiences varying from the wonder of the Show Cave to what has become familiarly known as 'creepy crawly caving' or wet caving. Leonie's piece of writing (p.90) offers an accurate description of the routines and, true to her personality, she maintains control of her feelings. We are offered an insight into the sense of trepidation caused by this sort of new experience when she tells us 'my heart began to beat fast' and again 'it was pitch black it was like a black cloak over our heads'.

Wet caving.

To go caving we had to wear a hat with a light on an old jumper and some old trousers. We wore a red cagoule as well. On our feet we wore our wellingtons and thick socks when the other group came back we got in the van and drove off to Thistle cave when we got there we had to walk for a bit to get to the cave, The cave was in a field we had to line up. When we were outside the cave Mark gave us a number I was number 8 this was to see if every one was in the cave if number 17 didn't call his number out that meant he was lost. In the cave we turned on our lights, as Mark went inside the cave my heart began to beat fast — at last it was my turn to crawl through the crack. Once we were all inside the cave we jumped down a rock and started to walk I was excited. We had to jump over another Rock then we had to walk through some water, Then Mark sat down and so did we. He told us to turn off our lights to see what it was like we turned them off and listened to the sounds of the cave Mark said "now you know what it's like to be a blind person." It was pitch black it was like a black cloak over our heads. Then we turned our lights back on we turned back and came to a worm hole Mark said that in the worm hole you had to make worm noises he said worm noises were saying things like "this is magic" "this is exciting" and it was. I thought the tunnel would never end but at last it did we sat down and waited untill everyone was out of the tunnel. Then we walked out of the cave and mark told us to turn our lights off. I thought that was the best experience ever.

Wet caving by Leonie, aged nine

For some children, the routine can be as much an adventure as the planned experience. Mark's poem (opposite) captures both the preparation for a visit to Yordas cave and his feelings in the cave itself. The cave is supposedly named after a giant, Yorda, and, as the children listen to the legend, candles are lit. These illuminate the walls and children are encouraged to use their imaginations about what they can see. Other parts of the cave have names, for example the jewellery box, so called because of the colours of the rocks. The cave is vast, damp and very dark. The children can walk under the waterfall which is usually torrential. The cave offers a wonderful sensory experience whilst retaining an aura of mystery.

In a very few lines, the poem by Mark, aged nine, captures all the happenings of the day. His use of language and his style present a breathtaking race through what was for him a very new experience. It seems to signify relief from what is intended as a challenge, but, as many adult colleagues can testify, a rather testing ordeal for some!

```
YORDAS

Get the towel
Get changed
Go down the cellar
Wellies on with your cagoules on
now your helmet with no light.  Yes with no light
Up the steps we go
Shout hooray.  Out of doors
Photo taken in the minibus
Sing, all clap your hands and shout hooray
Going up the hillside, There at last
Through the entrance
How dark can you get.
I beg you to switch your lights on
No we won't
Now we hear swish splash swish
I think I can hear a waterfall
Yes you can but feel the rocks
Fall in the mud
Mucky now.  Help me up, thank you
Now go through a waterfall
Go through another gap
Put our candles in a circle
Sing happy birthday to Yordas
Play a game and back on the trail
Bang my head
In Yordas jewellry box
down a rock and up a trickle
I can see daylight, can you?  can you?
and my wellies are like a swimming pool
Out we go
Hooray, Hooray, back to the Hall
Hooray Hooray
Have a shower and then get changed
```

Yordas by Mark, aged nine

Melanie, aged eight, went to the same cave but during the summer. Her treatment of the same experience (p.92) is a very frank and honest account of the day. It was a very hot day, as she says, and the effort needed to reach the cave was great. Melanie never left anyone in doubt about how she felt about things and this occasion was no exception.

The reader could be forgiven for thinking that Melanie did not enjoy school visits, but on the same weekend as our visit to Yordas cave Melanie also visited the Show Cave. It was an evening experience and the children carried coloured lanterns through the cave. Back in school it took her just fifteen minutes to write the first draft of the poem on p.93. The redraft dealt only with presentation: she did not alter the content.

For anyone who has not visited the Show Cave before, it should be said that it can evoke differing images. Mark's treatment of the same visit (p.94) shows how he chose descriptive narrative to convey the impact it made on him. Both children shared the same experience and both children chose which genre they felt could best express their knowledge, thoughts and feelings. Both are effective pieces of writing, written by children who truly see themselves as confident, competent authors.

Evenings at Ingleborough Hall are precious and we hold many lasting memories of music, stories and dramas we have shared around the log fire. The legend of the Witch

Kingdale and Yodos. cave

Judy Mr Miller Mrs Bean and Mrs pollard were looking after us John holt And Anthony walker were helping us too All the kids were clumped up into Judys white van. Mr Miller and Judy were in the frontseats I Was one of the kids Who was clumped up in the Back. The journey in the Van was not very long we climed a Big hill my toes were gripping in My boobs Because the hill was very slopy we were only harlf way up the hill and we were shatterd Sweat Began to appear on My hot forehead we stoped for lunch By a stream Nearly everybody paddled except the rotten teachers who just Boringly talked and sunbathed the spoil sports. we lazily Ate lunch I had Refreshing orange-curd sandwitches And a big Carton of Orange then off we went again climbing hills Walking Until we Nearly collapsed as usual on Friday we almost died of thirst at last we Reached the Van we sunk into our Seats And put a Special hat on Because we were going caveing We had to stand with our hand on the person in fronts shoulder And walk in pitch Black with our Other hand on the wall the wall was Cold and Slymy We finaly got into the Cave and Judy Said how high do you think the Roof is? people had a few quessios Judy shone her light in the direction of the Roof it was realy high up. We Continued to walk We Came across a waterfall when you went near it, it Splashed against your face then there was a Bit of an Opening out we went And Back to the Van What arelifs!

Kingsdale and Yodos Cave by Melanie, aged eight

of Clapham features heavily in many of our visits. One exciting experience is a night walk through the grounds with the children carrying coloured lights. Again, the connotations of night and darkness and things 'spooky' create an electric atmosphere.

Another valuable activity combines music, story or poetry and imagination. We believe that music can help develop imagination in the following ways:

a)   it provides children with a problem-solving challenge;
b)   it does not present a visual picture as a photographer would but sounds made by a child on a musical instrument have to be interpreted as pictures in the child's or listener's mind;
c)   children trying to emulate environmental sounds which they have heard will often substitute sounds produced on musical instruments for those naturally produced or will experiment with a combination of musical sounds in order to achieve a matching timbre.

When children write stories or poetry you can bring them to life and extend them through the introduction of music − not in the sense of purely playing or adding sound effects, but in the creation of the atmosphere and character of the story itself.

Sounds have tremendous possibilities for the creation of atmosphere. It is important that children develop this sound awareness as early as possible. It can add a new dimension to storywriting. It is natural for children to combine the two. Think of examples from incidental music in films and TV used in different ways to express feelings. Children pick up on this and, if given the opportunity, will usually take to the work with great sensitivity.

CAVING

Stalactites dangling from the roof in mingled shapes like forests upside down

The beehives shaped by chemicals in water so spectacular how they form

Walking, seeing the wet still shaped walls looking at you.

The meek witch's fingers dangling, frightening, dangling over your head

The sad tears drip dropping to bring some poor child sorrow.

Look into the pool of reflection

See a wonderous fairy's castle gleaming there to show off.

The great stubby elephants leg crumpled up against a wall — not very tall

Horses leg and hoof stands looking so life like — not a bit like stone

The clear, cool ice pool deadly

Jump in and freeze for fifteen seconds and then die.

Night lights gleaming different colours

Walking

Your candles flickering in the depths of the show cave

As scary as it is. Oh everyone knows.

Clawed, ravished curtains hanging in shreads

The coffee pot waiting for steaming hot coffee to be poured into its lair

The bold, big jockey's hat just sitting on the floor

Welcome to the wonderous wonderland of stone.

Caving by Melanie, aged eight

Often, children are not given this chance. They may be given an instrument or two and allowed to play but in most cases they have already been conditioned in the ways the instruments are to be used.

We, as teachers, often stifle children's natural exploration in music by restricting the use of instruments, and conforming to traditions and recognised ways of playing instruments.

The show cave

In the show cave mark from the hall told us about a crystal pool but what he didn't tell us that if we fell in we would die in 15 seconds because it was so cold. It was so cold because it had never seen daylight. The mushroom bed we saw next. The mushroom bed is a massive bank of stalagmite formation with a rippled effect on its surface due to miniature runstone pools Ridges of lime holding back pools with minute crystals of lime on them. The water level is a white line on the wall we walked on and came to the horses leg. The horses leg is a stalactite formation we walked foward and looked to our right and there was a coffee-pot not a real one a stalagmite formation. Then we came to the witches finger with tears dripping from it. Then we came to where we had to crawl. I was absolutely petrified when we had crawled through. We had the night lights they were burning brightly in the darkness of the cave we walked along a dark spooky passage with the night lights we came to a long pool of water which was called the pool of reflection in it was a hidden fairy castle with towers of gold and fairy flags of pure white how lovely it would be to live in a under water city with a fairy castle with towers of gold and fairy flags of pure white. the elephants leg so stubborn and short the elephants leg is a stalactite and a stalagmite joined together when the Join they are called colums. stalactites grew down and stalagmites grow up on our way back we saw skittle Alley skittle Alley is a big group of stalagmites growing up when we had nearly reached the cave Entrance I saw a bat it was Quite small and fast eventually we reached the end

The Show Cave by Mark, aged nine

Encourage the creative use of instruments, and at the same time establish a relationship of caring. We need to really open up music and imagination and allow children the experience of experimentation and sound awareness. If we do not allow this freedom early on, composition and creativity become far more difficult.

Teachers should aim to move away from total direction to more interpretation and open imagination. Children who have never approached this work do not really know the bounds. Once they begin to think, the teacher can take more of a back seat. Only through this kind of approach can true imagination and creativity develop – and they will!

The important process is working together and sharing ideas and imaginative experiences. In this way, children will take on the role of producer and critic.

With music, story and imagination we have just touched the surface of atmosphere. The connection between music and story can be far greater. Movement, dance and song all have their part. Stories can be further developed in three ways:

- incidental (atmospheric)
- characterisations (leitmotifs)
- songs

If the interest in sounds and sound pictures can begin at four to five years and creativity and extension is allowed through school, there is no reason why children cannot move easily into song composition as part of their story extravaganza.

The natural way of extending musical stories once the incidental music is there is to add a poem or make a song. A musical is then the next development – once planning is done.

Building on this belief, we planned a night walk having prepared the children back in school about the legend of Alice Kettyl, the Witch of Clapham. Children wrote poems and we selected the following, for which we felt we could create musical accompaniment.

In a spooky wood is a ruined castle –there lives a witch

Foggy, shadowy, as black as pitch, is the terrible wood where lives the witch

Swirling mists as the cauldron boils

Anyone who enters that wood will be a slave who forever toils

On midsummers night every year.

That terrible witch suddenly

APPEARS.

Poem on the Witch of Clapham by Andrew, aged nine

Sixty children and ten adults armed with a variety of instruments, body parts, and features in the Hall, for example radiators, the floor, the bannister etc. practised making music. The finale resulted in the culmination of a feast of music, poetry and imagination.

Another strategy we have adopted is to create a problem or role play situation which means that the children become engaged in a problem-solving weekend. This requires preparation with staff at the Hall and depends on 'the problem' being plausible enough for the children to be convinced it is real.

We prepared a script on 'parchment', supposedly from the witch, saying that unless twelve items were found, including 'a sign of life from the cave of the dead man', 'a single sede from the wylde wood' and a 'spoonful of earth taken in secret from the reflecting pool', Ingleborough Hall would have to close.

The children believed the role play and spent the afternoon using the reference material and maps in an attempt to discover where to find the items. On the following day the quest began. The experience was an excellent way of using language for communication. In the evening the children presented their 'treasures' to each other,

Thriller Cave by Joanne, aged nine

seated quietly around a group of candles in a darkened room. The atmosphere was electric. Later, Joanne, aged nine, who had been in the group looking for 'the spoonful of earth from the reflecting pool' in the Show Cave produced the poem above.

Searching for the 'earth' had not detracted from the experience of wondering at the splendour of the cave.

Residential experiences can offer the stimulus for writing for different purposes. As long as we do not adopt the strategy of demanding over-directed pieces of writing but, instead, allow children the freedom to decide how best they would like to portray their thoughts and feelings, then we will be rewarded with work of excellent quality. Also, we should allow time for the irrational subconscious processes of the mind to work. We like De Bono's (1967) analogy of capturing and pinning a butterfly in order to illustrate how human beings tend to pounce on an idea and drag it into full consciousness before it has had the chance to grow and take shape. The shape is one that has been chosen for the idea, not one it might have grown into on its own.

7 The Persuasive Aims of Writing

Of all the uses of language and discourse, persuasion features perhaps the most frequently (Kinneavy 1971). Indeed, persuasion has become an everyday part of life as children and adults alike are faced constantly with having to evaluate and make choices on a whole range of issues. Arguments may be backed by evidence or simply the emotional way an argument is presented may be enough to effect the persuasion. Certainly, presentation is a key element in any persuasion but there is no one form of presentation that suits all situations and all audiences. The approach may vary considerably, being determined very much by the issue and the people involved. Should we go and play on the swings or out on our bicycles? Should we buy brand X or brand Y soap powder? Which is the better? There is no age limit to effecting persuasion and indeed very young children are often found in situations listening to evidence, providing opposing views and making emotional statements in favour of something they firmly believe in. For many parents making demands upon their children the little words 'why', 'but', and 'what if' can be very frustrating as they are often forced into a defensive position by children eager to persuade their parents to alter their point of view. Persuasion and argument at this level, viewing situations and arguing purely from a personal, egocentric stance are surely as natural to young children as fantasy and make-believe.

The art of persuasion can be a much longer, more complex process resulting from a combination of many facets of logic, thought and discourse form. To persuade somebody is the end-product of this process which, as children develop, can involve careful planning, the gathering of evidence, the checking of facts, the making of emotional and value-laden statements, the justifying of arguments, and generally the pressing of one point of view at the expense of those in opposition. While walking past groups of children in a playground, it will become obvious that many young children can and do argue quite naturally using some of these skills, holding and justifying points of view and persuading others to agree to a variety of issues that are pertinent at that particular time. Involving the same children in an organised classroom discussion, however, may fail to elicit the same fluency and power of persuasion as witnessed in the less formal playground situation. The question must be raised, 'What do we as teachers do to restrict children in the natural extension of their powers of persuasion and argument in the classroom?' Perhaps we ask them to discuss and argue issues that lack personal meaning, interest or indeed relevance. Perhaps we create an environment or atmosphere that intimidates children and discourages the honest expression of feelings, or perhaps we have implicitly laid down classroom rules and an understanding that only certain children and opinions have value.

If this is the case, it not surprising that writers in Wilkinson (ed.) (1986) and Bereiter and Scardamalia (1982, 1985) suggest that young children may find persuasive writing so difficult. Not only must they decentralise their own thinking, listen to and perhaps write opposing views to their own, but they often have to do this without real opportunities to share emotional argument and persuasive discourse in open discussion in the classroom. Most primary teachers do see the value of discussion and will encourage a certain amount of it. As a means of introducing a written task, discussion does play a big part in the primary classroom, but often the discussion will come to an abrupt end with the words 'Now go and write about it.' How often do we as teachers have the courage to continue and support discussion and debate until it reaches its natural conclusion? Perhaps over-preponderance upon a product-orientated system or anxiety that the headteacher will walk into a room and question why the children are not 'working' does somewhat determine the length and level of discussion in the classroom context. The need to maintain and allow for extended discussion however should not be underestimated as it is through this that children learn to question, argue and evaluate evidence, so important in the development of persuasive writing. Persuasive writing is indeed a natural extension of discussion and its structure relies heavily upon the dialogue form. Speech provides opportunity for thoughts, ideas and arguments to be formulated and is therefore a central vehicle for children to develop and argue opinions and points of view on a topic or issue, constantly extending and adding a more complex perspective upon it (Dixon and Stratta in Wilkinson (ed.) 1986).

For persuasive writing to develop, opportunities need to be provided for children to offer opinion and equally discuss arguments and counter-evidence without intimidation, in an environment that values and does not demean or stifle the contributions of individuals. The establishing of such an environment and forum for discussion is the essential foundation required if persuasive writing is to develop beyond spoken dialogue and into the written form.

The step between persuasive argument in spoken discourse and in the written form is huge. Whereas young children may confidently express views and consider the rights and wrongs of an argument when actually involved in dialogue with another person, in writing persuasive and argumentative essays the conversational partner is absent and therefore the writer must be able to justify his or her own arguments and also those of an imaginary opponent. It is this sudden transfer from persuasion as a two-way dialogue to persuasion as a self-initiated mixture of opinions and imagined responses, with a greater need for forward planning, that young children find so difficult. It is therefore not surprising that some children continue to heavily emphasise the dialogue form in their written essays (p. 100).

In bridging this gap between spoken and written argument, it is therefore the teacher that must take on the role of the dialogue partner and support the child's line of thought and argument through the giving of cues, reassurance and general conferencing as outlined in Chapters One and Three. Through teacher-support in this way, and an emphasis upon persuasion as an exploration of the issues and the diversity of thought rather than persuasion as a confrontation between two adversaries, the extension of opinion essays and persuasive writing should become the natural development of classroom

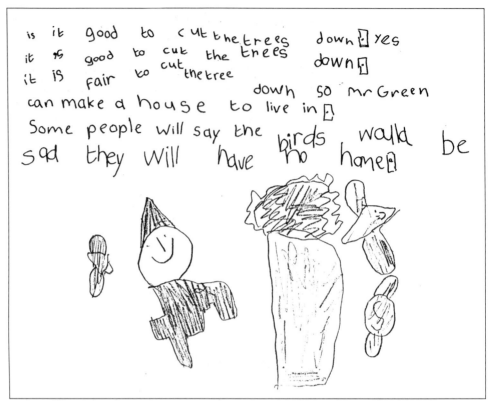

is it good to cut the trees down? yes
it is good to cut the trees down.
it is fair to cut the tree
down so Mr Green
can make a house to live in.
Some people will say the birds wald be
sad they will have no home.

Writing in dialogue form by Yusef, aged five

discussion. Children talking and working together on written tasks can provide a forum for the sharing of different perspectives upon an issue or theme. If tackled in this way, exploring the positive and negative points of each argument, issues that are relevant to the children can be discussed without fear of intimidation or ill-feeling. Dixon and Stratta (in Wilkinson (ed.) 1986) identify a number of features in argumentative opinion essays that will illustrate children's greater control of the style and form of persuasive writing.

1. Attitudes, opinions and general statements supported by well-grounded evidence;
2. A more flexible view of the range of consequences and implications;
3. A social ability to engage with readers with varying attitudes, opinions and values;
4. An awareness of the demands of the reader, thus a willingness to offer explicit cues as to rationale, coherence and overview;
5. A willingness to qualify generalisations and reformulate proposals;
6. An ability to relate personal experience to broader public knowledge which has been critically reviewed.

Already, by the age of five, Yusuf is beginning to show some of the qualities identified by Dixon and Stratta, not as the result of a 'one-off' experiment, but as a result of a whole approach that recognises the importance of a number of features in the development of persuasive thought and writing:

1. incorporating regular opportunities for open and often extended discussion and the sharing of opinions in an environment that values and encourages the contributions of all children;
2. ensuring that issues introduced into this forum are issues of immediate interest and concern to the children involved and are not contrived purely to enable persuasive discourse to take place. Such issues should come from the children and in so doing will have real purpose and meaning to the participants;

3. encouraging children to work collaboratively, evaluating facts and arguments in the discussion, planning and the writing of persuasive prose;
4. teacher encouragement and support to children entering into and developing writing of a persuasive nature, providing them with a dialogue partner and cues not only to help extend thinking on the issue but to help organise and structure thoughts or arguments when required.

If the above features are incorporated into classroom practice then persuasive writing is not beyond the capabilities of young children. The following projects outline how issues that grew from the children's interest and experience developed opportunities for persuasive writing with six- to eight-year-old children. In all cases the above features were an established part of the classroom ethos and children had been used to persuasive argument and the oral evaluation of evidence and opinion. The children worked in an environment where co-operation rather than competition was a central feature and where all children felt able to offer opinions and suggestions knowing that they would be valued, not dismissed or ignored.

Case study: Playtimes

A group of eight- to nine-year-olds had been involved in a topic on redesigning the playground. Inevitably the issue of playtime arose and, playing the devil's advocate, the teacher told the children of a conversation in the staffroom about whether playtimes are a good thing or a bad thing. After much discussion, the children were asked to prepare their case in answer to the suggestion, 'the teachers are thinking about not having any playtime any more. How do you feel about this?' They planned first and then wrote opinion essays. The examples show the confidence with which the children tackled the subject matter. They were able to generate text without a respondent, a task which proves demanding for more mature writers.

Natalie's writing (p.102) is marked by very commendable traits. She maintains the thread of her argument throughout and the reader is made very clear about how she feels about the subject. There are many 'I thinks', and she gives examples followed by opinions, 'I think that's unfair'. Her concluding sentence also provides an excellent summary.

Children need to write opinion essays in order to learn how to write opinion essays. Quality will develop through use of this strategy coupled with exposure to much reading and listening to other people's opinions.

Writing about a topic such as playtime leads to a greater length of essay since this issue is very personal to the children. This allows the children to produce extended discourse autonomously, especially since a guiding adult may not always be there after each idea is written. The subjective nature of this topic helped the children to recognise and cope with structural problems that arose. Another important issue which affects the quality of the writing is preparation. If children are well prepared before writing and know they can discuss their work during the composing process if they so wish, then this procedure plays a facilitating role enabling them to produce writing of both quality and quantity as the piece by Joanne (aged nine) illustrates (pp. 103-4).

> The teacher's are thinking about not having any play time any more
>
> How do you feel about this?
>
> I think we should have playtime's because we need the fresh air but sometimes I'm a bit bored because the boys are always playing football and they take up all the room. I think we should have a big improvement to are school playtime. I think we should have a few climbing frames and a few slides I think we should have a drink because the teacher's always have a hot cup of tea or coffee I think that's unfair. I think it's fair if the teacher's stayed out in the freezing cold while we go in and have a drink. Its alright in summer but still the teacher's stay in the staffroom and chat and have a drink. Sometimes they a lot of bullying going on and some people always spoil the fun like the morkey ones and the naughty ones I think they's no reason at all to stop having playtime's. The only teacher that stays out in the cold is Mr. walker. The teachers are always slow at getting up from the staffroom. The biggest problem is Mr. walker always sends you out five minutes after the bell has gone. The teacher's would want a break to get away from the children and they ed feel much better after a break. I think the children and the teacher's need a playtime as much as each other.

Writing about playtime by Natalie, aged eight

When children attempt essays which are concerned to present alternative viewpoints, style can be affected and the writing becomes halting and uncertain. This is not to be viewed as wrong, but rather we should understand that the writing task becomes a heuristic one, a process of discovery and reformulation as opposed to a finished piece which results in a more fluent style of writing. Asha's essay (on p.105) illustrates this point.

Asha is concerned to present alternative viewpoints but as a consequence her style is affected. Her writing is dominated by a complex network of ideas which is rich in arguments and counter-arguments, yet which leads to a rather awkward style. When children struggle with the demands of presenting two alternative viewpoints it is analogous to the high diver who opts to perform a high tariff dive. If the dive is successful, s/he will score highly – however, if the execution is not quite right, s/he will be marked down. In the case of the diver who opts for a low tariff dive, chances

The teachers are thinking about not having playtime anymore How do you feel about this?

Playtimes are good fun and I don't think that teachers should stop them.

You need the fresh air at playtime because it gets hot and stuffy in the classroom.

At playtime you have a chance to talk to your friends especially those in other classes.

At playtime you can play good games the boys play football but the girls play things like elastic and they skip and some play with whip and tops.

Playtime gives you a chance to have somthing to eat like a bag of crisps or a biscuit or somthing like that.

I don't think that playtimes should be stopped because the children enjoy them and when the top classes go on to the middle school they will only get a playtime in the morning so why should we stop them here, yes but think of ~~thank of~~ the children who are cold lonely and bored at playtime and have no friends to talk

Writing about playtime by Joanne, aged nine

of success are greater, but is it not the diver who attempts the more difficult dive who commands greater respect and who is considered to be more expert?

The sooner children are exposed to a variety of genres the more they will learn about them. Novice writers beginning to write in an unfamiliar genre, for example persuasive writing, will experience difficulties. However, as teachers we should encourage critical thinking from an early age for, as Frank Smith (1982, p.108) suggests,

When we both have something to say and the will to say it, then the mechanism engages and the words come. We speak up (or write down).

Young children do possess the confidence to voice opinions on all manner of things and are not afraid to 'tell it as they see it'. They are aware of issues such as gender and are very capable of analysing the 'pros and cons' of the situation.

to how will they feel? I know but if they want a friend why don't they go and get one there are lots of other children hanging around who want a friend anyway I've made my point clear and I don't think that playtimes should stop. Anyway the teachers have a playtime don't they even if they just go into a warm room and have a warm drink the children can always run around and get warm can't they I think that playtimes are good fun for the children and that there good for the teachers because they will want a chat because they have been working just as hard as the children. And If we do stop playtimes the children will probably get more work done and they will get the hang of work because they are not going out for quarter of an hour.

Writing about playtime cont.

An important aspect in the facilitation of writing is the motivational factor of wanting to say something. Equally important as a means of eliciting good writing may indeed be the genuineness of the task. In the school situation, opportunities in which there is a real need to offer a persuasive argument should be seized.

Persuasive writing, by its nature, calls for a co-ordination of the cognitive with emotional and imaginal approaches. What children choose to write makes sense because it is rooted in a complex net of feelings and attitudes. Hearts as well as minds will be involved. Through persuasive writing, we come to know the child more fully for, as Harrison (1983, p.83) tells us:

pieces of writing tellingly reveal who their creators *are,* and what their experience of the world *is* (not who or what they 'ought' to be).

The Teachers are thinking
about not having playtimes anymore
how do you feel about this?

I think we should stop playtimes
I don't because children have lots of fun at playtime and would not like
to stay in. well there are lots of children that don't like playtimes and would
like to stay in because they get cold and its not very nice to be cold.
and anyway there is to much sighting at playtimes. at playtimes when we are
sighting we are having fun and no one gets hurt relly and there are more
people that would like to stay out than go inside and nobody wants to stay
in over summer as well as winter and if you stop playtimes then in
the summer when everybody wants to go out nobody will be able
to go out so why don't you do something els for these people
so they are not cold like leting them have a warm drink like you
teachers I don't see why teachers should have a warm drink and
not let children have a warm drink. well there is not so much for all
the school to have some, well made some because you don't want
them to be cold and you can stay in the warm but the cold
people go out where people are kicking sighting teasing play hidders
playing scootball and lots of uther things but I still think we should
have playtimes because it's fun and why not let the cold people
and board people go outside for a bit of fresh air and then
let them come in for the rest of play. well if we do that
they will still be board because there will have nobody to play
with they can play with the uther people that are board. nobody
will be able to look after them they can be looked after like
at indoor plays but all in the same classroom so you don't
need a teacher in every classroom

Writing about playtime by Asha, aged nine

Case study: Should tourists be allowed in Robin Hood's Bay?

Shells, seaweed and gulls

During an extended visit to Whitby with a class of seven- to eight-year-old children, a day was spent in Robin Hood's Bay, a village south of Whitby, exploring both the village and community, the famous rock pools and the coastline itself. The aim had been to compare animal life and habitation researched and identified in and around Bradford with animal life found and identified on the coastline. It was anticipated that follow-up work would centre around the marine life found in the rock pools, with the children spending time identifying creatures and observing the variety of life present, in line with the Science National Curriculum Statements of Attainment and Programmes of Study. The village and its coastline were also to be highlighted, particularly the building styles and materials and their similarities and differences with those seen in Bradford. In reality, the concentration of work moved away from the structure of the village and the marine life of the bay towards the community, the environment and the many problems that community and environment face each year as the tourist season begins.

Understanding the community

Following the visit to Robin Hood's Bay, it became clear by the children's written reports of the visit that not only had the rock pools formed a highlight of the day but a number of other features had also created interest and were well represented in the children's work. Perhaps some chance remark had stimulated thought or the actual visual experience had generated real curiosity. Whichever the case, features that were frequently highlighted in the children's work included the traffic problem in the village and the amount of litter and pollution witnessed around the village and the bay. The village is built on the side of a steep cliff, and the only car park is a small area on the cliff top. During the walk through the village the children had witnessed first-hand the problems of cars passing each other on the narrow, winding streets in the village. Often, cars would have to reverse under very difficult conditions as delivery vans and tourists blocked the road. A house on a street corner, demolished by a runaway vehicle several weeks prior to the visit, dominated discussion on the way down to the beach and became a key point in written work that followed. Litter and pollution on the beach caused deep concern among the children as they stumbled against plastic bags and tin cans. Information that the already eroding cliffs were made worse by tourists digging in the soft cliffs for fossils, fossils being an important feature of the bay, also heightened a general concern for the environment.

Discussion of these points was encouraged as children, showing genuine concern, developed argument and debate over the whole issue of tourists and their effect upon the community of Robin Hood's Bay. The children were initially damning of tourism and all were clear in their argument, exhibiting different levels of understanding, and were keen to share these arguments with a trusted audience. All children listened and extended their arguments in written form, some independently and others with the support of Breakthrough Sentence Makers. The written arguments were pinned together and displayed so that an overview of the many points and arguments could be seen by all concerned. Cars not only caused congestion but also damaged the environment. Tourists created noise and pollution, upsetting residents and causing actual damage to the bay itself. The points made by the children covered all the issues and a real case against allowing tourists into the village was made.

Providing a balanced view

The arguments were certainly one-sided but, after sharing them with the class, dialogue was extended further by focusing in upon the positive contribution tourism made in the area. Children had to think deeply and offered suggestions as to why some members of the community welcome tourism. Gift shops, cafés and some jobs connected with car parking and litter collection would no longer be required if tourists were banned from the village. The initial negative view of tourism was therefore balanced by the positive and children began to reason why tourism could be good for the village and the positive effect it could have upon people. Residents would want their village and their houses to look nice for the visitors and would keep the village clean and tidy. Tourists would spend their money in the village, etc. Dialogue and discussion were further encouraged and, through the sharing and exploration of both sides of the tourism argument, children were encouraged to extend their thoughts into the written form by producing a series of arguments and counter-arguments for tourists being allowed to visit Robin Hood's Bay (opposite).

Solving the problems

The implications of a tourist ban and the practicalities of enforcing it were also discussed openly and children soon began to realise the problems this would entail. Therefore the initial problems and issues which had been identified by the children

Some people don't like people at the seaside because the leave litter on the beech.
Sometimes they help tidy the beech and make it look nice.
They sometimes make the cliffs fall down and are silly and throw things at the creatures. Some people like people at the seaside to have new fiends and it is nice on the beech with sand castles and people like to sell icecrem and buckets and spades and they wont sell them and will be poor if no one goes.

Writing about tourists at Robin Hood's Bay by Teresa, aged seven

were again highlighted and they were left to ponder and devise ways of overcoming the problems of noise, pollution, traffic and car parking in the bay without enforcing a total ban on tourism. Environmentally-friendly car parks were designed and constructed, written explanations accompanying them (p.108). Methods of curbing noise were experimented with, litter-collection systems were designed and anti-erosion devices designed, built and tested in a simulation tank in the classroom.

Following the initial experience, real concern and opinions were shared openly by the children. Opinions which were very much 'anti-tourism' were challenged as the teacher tried to balance discussion and provide alternative points of view. These suggestions led naturally to the children challenging many other arguments they themselves had made. Therefore, from an initial, negative, view of tourism, discussion opened the children's attitudes and provided an ideal forum for debate and persuasive discourse. Where the children's initial comments were one-sided, failing to appreciate alternative views, the teacher was able to introduce a balanced view by opening up discussion of the issues and encouraging the children to analyse their own thinking. When the children accepted this and further questioned the arguments they themselves had made, they were able to allow the establishment of counter-arguments with equal value to their own. The sharing of counter-evidence and argument in this way had not only helped to develop the children's power of persuasive argument through the exploration of different opinions and views, but had also developed their understanding of negotiation and collaboration as part of the process involved in the development of persuasive writing.

I think you should keep the seaside very tidy. You need a carpark near the sand because there is too much traffic in Robin Hoods Bay and the people who go to visit the seaside leave litter behind so that people who live there have to pick it up. It is not fair on them and the cars that park there leave oil behind or lead and they leave it all over the place.

I made a carpark and the first thing I had to do was to measure the wood and it was 49 cm and 11 cm. I used some cardboard and then I got two toilet rolls and two little toilet rolls. I used the rolls for the cars to get in and out of the carpark. I put two more toilet rolls from the top floor of the carpark to the beach to let people slide down onto the beach. One side goes to the top floor and the other side goes to the bottom floor. By putting the carpark inside the cliff it stops the cars messing the place and making a lot of noise.

Writing about making a car park at Robin Hood's Bay by Elaine, aged seven

Case study: Frogspawn

We were invited to take part in an amphibian study by our local Countryside Warden and this meant raising children's awareness as to the habitats and lifestyles of various creatures. We visited local sites in an attempt to identify species and to consider which kind of water, e.g. flowing, stagnant, shallow, deep etc. provided the most suitable habitat. The children took photographs and recorded the data on computer as well as publishing the results for the rest of school. They sent the information to the national project whose brief it was to keep an amphibian watch. During this work issues of care and concern for the environment and living creatures were raised.

The Countryside Warden told the children of his concern that so many people were helping themselves to frogspawn that he felt there was a possibility of it becoming an endangered species. He described how some children had helped him move lorry loads of spawn to new breeding grounds. Since the practice in many schools is to collect frogspawn for the children to watch its cycle, the Warden queried this with the children especially in the light of the concerns about too much being removed.

Much discussion ensued and it was decided to hold a debate in order to address this issue. The outcome would affect whether we brought frogspawn into our classroom and this would have implications for policy in the rest of school. The children were asked to prepare their case. We agreed that the title would be:

'Is it right to take frogspawn away from its natural environment? How do you feel about this?'

Here are two alternative viewpoints:

I think that it is a good idea to keep frogspawn in the class as long as they put it back because it could die in the class. When they are frogs they could jump out and jump all over. If we did not have the real thing we could not learn and you can learn the frog cycle. We should look after them. If someone disagreed they would say you get more information in books, but I think it is better to have the real thing. They will die if they don't have the proper temperature and their own water. There should be signs saying 'Be careful. Frogs cross roads day and night. Frogs need space too.'

Peter (aged eight)

I think you should keep frogspawn in a pond because if they live in a fish tank they haven't got enough room to hatch and they have the proper food in a pond and they have more water. You can learn about frogspawn in your books. I think you should keep frogspawn in a pond because people poke at them and try to kill them in the classroom. If they ever do turn into frogs I think it's cruel to keep them in the class because they haven't got their own food and the temperature isn't right.

Nichola (aged eight)

8 The Referential Aims of Writing

The term 'referential' means simply 'that which is referring to something or is verifiable'. With regard to a balanced writing approach, the referential aim is writing that therefore refers specifically to some experience or issue the children have either witnessed or have been involved in. It is usually a factual account or report that contains specific information as opposed to narrative which is often imaginary. For example, the report of a museum visit, the writing up of traffic survey results, or the researching of specific plants or animals etc., are all aspects of work that require the reporting of facts. All these constitute referential writing. They give information, reports and are closely connected with reality either personally experienced by the children or gleaned from a variety of sources. In all the aims of writing identified by Kinneavy (1971) and illustrated in this book, there is much overlap. Indeed, many forms of writing include reference to some event whether it be persuasive writing connected to a real issue, expressive protest on some genuine environmental concern or a poem following a visit. Whereas reference to subject matter does not constitute the primary aim of literary, expressive or persuasive writing, in referential writing, it does. The production of factual accounts and first-hand descriptions become the main aim of the task.

Referential writing, juxtaposed with imaginative storywriting, takes perhaps the greatest share of all writing tasks tackled in primary schools and is frequently the first aim of writing to which most children are introduced. Children as young as five or six are commonly asked by the teacher to write their 'news' or report on an assembly or an experience they have been through together. The approach seldom changes and the philosophy held by many teachers is that by giving children more of the same, children will develop their skills in the referential form. This assumption regularly leads to children, on return from a school trip or visit, being given the task 'now go and write about it'. Such tasks often constitute the major, if not the only piece of writing stimulated by the actual experience. It is often seen as pure formality that every child relives the sequence of events experienced during an educational visit in written form, not with the purpose of sharing the experience with those unable to take part, but purely to let the teacher know how much the child has remembered. This may appear to be rather a cynical view of such tasks but the actual sequence of events on a visit often receives greater emphasis than children's personal feelings and experiences of the day and the depth of thought and style involved in the writing process following the visit (opposite).

Following a day trip, the teacher and children relived the sequence of events orally and were then left to write about the day. By talking through the sequence of the day's events, highlighting certain points, the teacher was implicity directing the children towards the key points of the visit as he saw them. Through this, he was actually determining what the children were to include in the piece. This continued even to the point of reading through the work with the child and asking the question 'did you enjoy it?' to which the child was obliged to answer in the form of a postscript.

Referential writing following the major experience of a school trip can be far more than this and need not be of the rehearsed and stilted nature illustrated in the example below. It can take many forms and can become a whole mixture of styles and purposes including sequenced events, descriptions, questions and thoughts all experienced as part of the day. Children will often remember or

Our Day Out by Paul, aged six

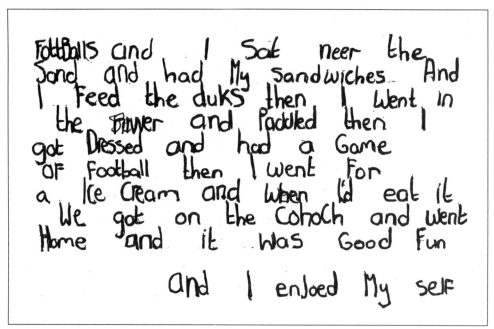

Our Day Out cont.

highlight points that were seen as being of minor importance by the teacher, but which become very important to the child. The coach trip may well have meant far more to the child than the actual visit itself and therefore, by allowing children flexibility in their writing and the opportunity to record their joint experience from a variety of personal viewpoints, the teacher is encouraging greater freedom, variety and ultimately greater depth in the children's written response.

The highlight of Paul's trip had been the game of football at Bolton Abbey. He was encouraged to discuss what happened in the game and why he had enjoyed it. Paul's second piece of writing on p.113 shows not only an excellent sequence of events but detail and personal writing style absent in his initial response.

Kinneavy (1971) identifies three different components under the heading of 'referential writing', each being specific but often combining together in order to fulfil the demands of a wider range of purposes and situations introduced to children as development takes place. Identified as being Exploratory, Informative, and Scientific, Kinneavy explains that where exploratory discourse asks a question, informative discourse answers the question and scientific discourse proves it. Related specifically to a writing task, therefore, a topic on buildings and building materials could begin with surveys on the materials used to construct houses in the community. Exploratory writing could discuss the results of the survey, the gathering of information and hypothesis on reasons why certain materials were used. This would continue into the proving of hypothesis through science experiments and the gathering of factual information as evidence to support the child's claim.

In this example, the three components of referential writing are seen as a sequence of the writing process from informative to the scientific. However, the three components do not consistently work together in this way and, under the umbrella term 'referential writing', emphasis may be purely upon

Mr Wagstaff gave Us a football and We went to sort out our teams. Mark tossed a penny and I won. I kicked the ball to Gavin and he ran down the wing. Mark tackled him so I chased after him. Mark was getting away but John ran behind and tackled him. oh No. Mark fell down. I got off after the ball. Darren got there before me. we ran down the pitch and there it was. It was me and Darren. His face was angry. I looked at him and we was both stood still looking at each other. Suddenly I ran forward and kicked the Ball away. John got the ball and Kicked it away. He passed it to me I ran with the Ball and there it was I Kicked it hard and. yes. it was a goal.

The Football Game by Paul, aged six

the scientific proving of hypotheses. It may equally exclude the scientific component and lay emphasis upon the stating of information in the form of instructions or the reporting of events. Similarly, exploratory writing in the form of research using library skills and the higher order reading skills of skimming and scanning, SQ3R etc., as a means of gathering information from a variety of sources, may not involve the scientific aspect of the term whatsoever. Therefore, referential writing tasks could involve all three components collectively or individual emphases within that. To maintain balance, it is important that opportunities are provided for children to extend writing in all three forms; consequently, the teacher must view referential writing in its broadest terms and not restrict opportunities to the traditional reporting tasks outlined earlier.

The projects outlined in this chapter view referential writing in its broadest terms and have therefore presented opportunities for children to write using each aspect of the term. The number and variety of referential writing tasks that can be presented to young children is vast. A number of key writing purposes are identified below as related to referential writing, in order to illustrate some of the possibilities and lines of development within this aim of writing.

a) *Reporting:* an event, school trip, experience etc.;
b) *Gathering information and making summaries:* using library and reading skills to glean information from several sources and combine it into the written form;
c) *Factual information from observed evidence:* following a science experiment, observational study of life forms;
d) *Questioning and solving problems:* design and exploration of a variety of solutions to a problem, the design of surveys and questions etc.

The list is not exhaustive but is meant as an introduction to some of the purposes requiring reference to a specific experience or some factual knowledge which can be developed naturally in the primary classroom. The components of exploratory, informative and scientific writing overlap and are well represented throughout the case studies. Some written work has been produced collaboratively and has included the gathering of factual evidence derived from both first-hand observation and second-hand knowledge. There has been room for experiment and the testing of hypotheses, and the extension of library and study skills has grown alongside written work being tackled by the children as required. Each project has grown genuinely from the children's real need and desire to write as a means of furthering their knowledge and personal understanding of a topic or experience new to them.

Case study: The school trip

Traditionally, the class trip has formed either the major stimulus to mark the beginning of a new class topic, the major focus of a term's work or the culmination and drawing together of the various elements as a topic reaches its conclusion. Despite recent legislation affecting the funding of school visits, the provision of such stimuli as part of an experimental approach to learning – an approach widely recognised as being good primary practice – is as valuable today as at any time. The days of an annual whole school exodus to the coast or the countryside during the summer term are long past and teachers really do have to justify any visit they are proposing. It is no longer enough to view a school trip as a 'one off' experience with a minimum of follow-up work. It is therefore essential that the educational potential of such a stimulus is fully realised and used to maximum effect. The argument that young children soon forget a trip or experience and therefore follow-up work loses its significance after a few days should not be an excuse but a challenge for teachers looking for ways of building upon the experience and extending the children's understanding and involvement in it. School visits and the first-hand experience they give to children can lead to a wealth of quality writing by children if opportunities, encouragement and time is given to them. As art-work captures the essence of the visit, so discussion and writing can capture the atmosphere and reveal a real understanding and depth of knowledge about the experience and what it personally meant to the children.

The major emphasis in written work, however, is often given to the reliving of the trip in terms of sequencing events and recalling the experiences undertaken. That all children relive the trip in this way is seen by many as an essential and valuable part of the children's writing development. Our argument is that, although retelling the story of a visit and the reporting of experiences in a factual way may be a useful, important feature sometimes, to force all children into the same mould every time a visit is written about restricts the individual, forcing a pattern of response that may not have particularly captured every child's imagination. It could fail to realise the full potential of the experience in terms of writing variety and development. However, if sufficient flexibility allowed children the freedom to follow up a visit or individual interests gained from it in a variety of ways, the whole process being viewed as collaborative, then the variety of work styles and content could be drawn together as personal views, feelings and memories under the umbrella of a single shared experience. Indeed, it needn't be that the class produces thirty reports that sequence the visit, thirty poems about the woodland walk and thirty descriptions of the fir cones found during the walk. A collective package of writing, showing both depth and variety and covering all aspects of the trip would provide not only a record of the experience, but a more detailed insight into the breadth of personal thoughts and feelings experienced by each individual.

Written work surrounding a school visit could take on a variety of forms and purposes and should be viewed as part of the whole process involved in the development of a project. A visit to a park as part of a topic on Autumn, for example, could involve children planning the trip, writing directions and routes to be taken during the visit, and the devising of a programme of events. It could involve children researching different life forms with the aim of having written reference material at their fingertips and may include detailed observations, sequencing, reports, poetry and expressive prose. It could even extend into the scientific analysis of samples and persuasive writing connected with vandalism and pollution they have witnessed first hand. Indeed, the possibilities are endless. Essentially, the school trip needs to offer children opportunities to write referentially in the broadest sense. Each trip needs to be treated individually and written tasks need to reflect this through the giving of different emphases, varied presentation and the highlighting of different purposes. By avoiding a set pattern of approach and task following each visit, the teacher ensures that children come to the experience afresh without any predetermined or rehearsed style and format in their writing which is so often evident in children's reporting of events on a school trip.

Our trip to Manningham Park

In planning a science-based topic around the theme of a park, incorporating forces, the variety of life, and the exploration of science, as part of work in accordance with the National Curriculum Science Statutory Orders, the teachers of two classes of six-to seven-year-old children decided to arrange a visit to a local park. The park had several different playground structures and a huge variety of animal, plant and bird life, including a large pond for the study of water insects. Children had done a great deal of preparation work and the trip was to form a general rounding off of the topic and the applying of knowledge and skills learned in the classroom.

The two classes worked in a shared, team-teaching situation and it was anticipated that when the children returned to school opportunity would be given for the children to write about the trip as they remembered it. One teacher particularly wanted to avoid the retelling and sequencing of events as outlined earlier, and wanted the follow-up work to reflect the individuality of the park and visit. The school camera was therefore taken and, throughout the trip, the teacher took photographs not purely of features in the park but of the children and their reactions as well. It was thought that the photographs would 'tell the story' and, when combined with the personal thoughts, observations and reports, would be compiled into a book showing the many personal as well as factual facets of the trip.

Sequencing events

Several days after the visit, the photographs were brought into the classroom and shared with the children. Discussion over the photographs rekindled interest in the trip as children laughed at themselves in the photographs and began to relate incidents captured on film, incidents they themselves had forgotten about. This renewed enthusiasm brought personal memories and experiences of the trip into the open and created a great deal of interest. The photographs were sequenced by the children as they remembered the order of the trip. The photographs were then fixed on to sheets of paper and left for children to take and write on. Some people wanted to write about the photographs, others wanted to write their memories of the trip.

The organisation was made flexible, with other activities available for children not wishing to participate. Children wishing to use the photographs were given free choice and encouraged to write. The results were mixed. Where some children had written purely a descriptive passage about the photograph as they saw it, others wrote about the feelings they had experienced when the photograph was taken.

Some children were asked to imagine what the characters in the photograph may have been saying or thinking at the time of taking the photograph. These were added as thought or speech bubbles and many of the photographs took on a new meaning as the characters were given thoughts and words. Some children shared their own thoughts, giving a clearer indication of their personal feelings and the visit's importance and meaning in their eyes.

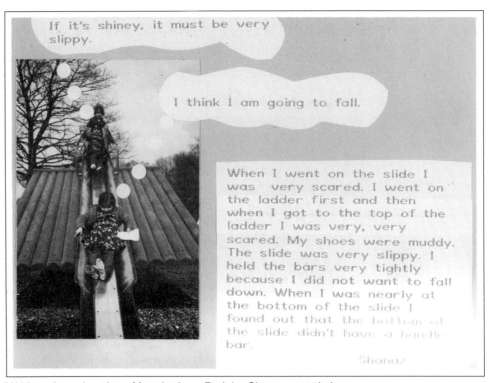

Writing about the trip to Manningham Park by Shanaz, aged six

Some photographs led to research as children wanted to identify the plants and birds captured on camera. Photographs of animal life in the park led to some children collaboratively researching factual information about the wildlife. Research, including drawing and illustration, was compiled and displayed alongside the written work and photographs.

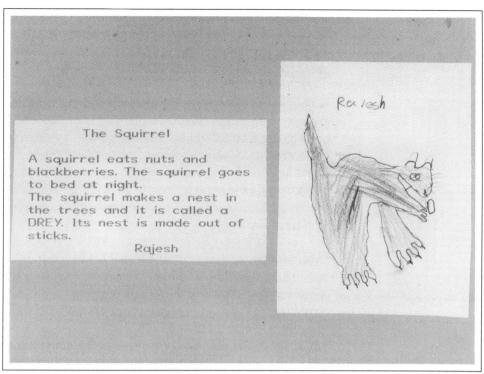

The Squirrel by Rajesh, aged six

The whole writing experience was drawn together, word processed by the children and teacher and bound into book form for all the children to share. It provides a visual sequence of the visit and a valuable mixture of emotions, descriptions and factual information written by the whole class of mixed ability children. Everybody's contributions were equally valued and displayed in the book. Work produced with the help of Breakthrough Sentence Makers was seen alongside written work produced independently. The book was shared with other classes and became a valuable reading resource for the school library and an individual record of an individual school trip.

A Whitby visit – devising reference material

As a class of seven- to eight-year-old children began to prepare for an extended visit to Whitby, discussion focused around an Ordnance Survey map of the area, tracing the routes and places of interest that were to be visited. The children had been used to using maps as part of the school's programme of environmental education and had been on many visits collecting data and research on animal and plant life in the environment. Several features were identified on the map where visits were to be made. These included the coast and village of Robin Hood's Bay, Dalby forest and the woodland trail of Littlebeck just south of Whitby. Discussion centred around these areas and the teacher was keen for the children to hypothesise using the information on the map as to the kinds of plant and animal life they might find during their visit. The children drew upon their previous experiences and were able to use the information they already had to suggest thoughts and ideas to the teacher.

It was suggested by a child that Usborne Spotter's Guide books, which were available in the classroom, could be taken on the trip to help identify creatures they might find. The limitations of this were immediately highlighted by the children. The class had only a very limited range of the books and therefore discussion about different alternatives ensued. A group decision was made by the children to write their own 'spotter's guides' and take them to Whitby themselves. A number of key subjects were chosen by the children and, either in isolation or in small groups, they began to search the library for information on the topic. Some chose to research seabirds, shells, wildflowers, trees and woodland creatures. One child chose seaweed and together the whole classroom became a hive of activity.

Although the skill of gathering information from a variety of books was not entirely new to the children, the problem of plagiarising information and abusing copyright in books was still apparent. Children were introduced to different coping strategies to try to overcome this. A number of key questions were devised by a group of children that would require reading but would then give a general picture of the creature they were researching. How big is it? Where does it live? What does it eat? etc. Children were encouraged to use a book's contents and index system and gather information in note form before writing.

Other strategies were introduced such as children being encouraged to glean and copy information from a number of sources. They were then encouraged to underline key points in the text and draw upon these key points when writing an article in their own words.

The absence of simple reference material did present problems for some children who, whilst keen to research and write about their subject, had difficulty reading the printed information available. By sharing the books with the teacher and parents in the classroom, the information was gathered. As much real evidence as possible was brought into the classroom for children to observe. Stuffed animals were borrowed from the local museum's service and children gradually began to build up a bank of information. Blank books were bound in school and the children, using writing and drawing materials, began to build up their own book, design the cover and devise the contents. Using the word processor, the books were professionally finished. In the production of a comprehensive series of factual 'spotter's guides' (opposite) for use on the trip, the children had gained a real understanding and insight into the environment of which they were to become a part and had been introduced to the extended reading skills as the genuine need arose.

Reporting to parents

The trip was a success and follow-up work covered a broad range of writing styles and purposes, all children working at their own pace and level on tasks and interests they themselves had negotiated with the teacher. It was decided to share a series of slides taken during the visit with parents as was customary after such a major venture. The slides were shown to the children one afternoon and it soon became obvious that the slides themselves did not provide the full atmosphere of the visit as children keenly added anecdotes and details of experiences, not captured on camera. The idea that the children could present the slide show and talk their way through the visit was supported by the teacher. Indeed, the whole slide sequence was accompanied by a prerecorded tape soundtrack. This package, including songs, music and a mass of written material and improvised dialogue, read by children, accompanied the slide show.

Parents were elated by the children's work and the obvious enthusiasm the visit had created among the children. The slide show is still used (two years on) as an introductory evening for parents of children going on the now annual Whitby trip. The concept epitomises the message of this book and is central to the very heart of our philosophy. Not only did the slide/tape presentation include a breadth of writing experience within it, but the project involved every child in the class presenting his

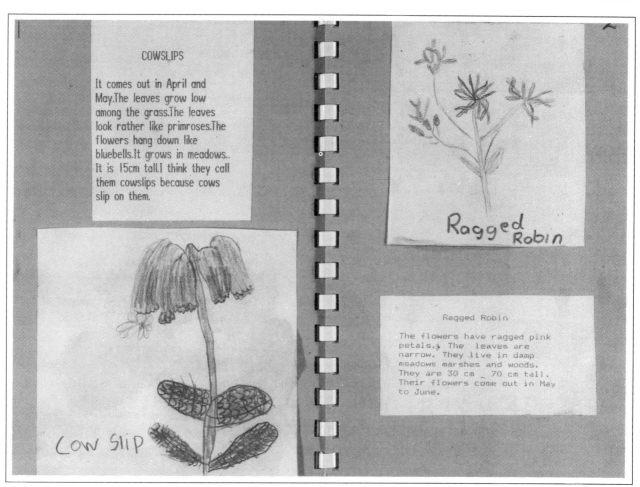

Spotter's Guide by Laura, aged eight

or her work alongside each other's and everyone working collaboratively on a task that had grown from a shared experience and developed into a child-controlled learning experience with real meaning and a genuine purpose behind it.

Case study: Stick insects

A class of eight- to nine-year-olds were given some stick insects. They remained in a cage for some time without too much interest being shown to them. While cleaning them out, however, a group of children became curious and started asking questions about these strange creatures. As the class teacher knew very little about stick insects, she encouraged the children to visit the library to search for information. This was the beginning of an exciting process which eventually led to the production of a pamphlet (pp.120-21).

In describing the processes which the children went through to produce the pamphlet we hope to be able to underline our firm belief that the best work is done when the child sees that the purpose is important to him or her. If a genuine requirement for information arises, then the use of reference books becomes less contrived. The most satisfactory work using books seems to be the situation which arises from a first-hand experience. Too often, the cry from teachers is that all children do when asked to write about a topic is to copy from a book.

This case study illustrates how skills can be more rapidly learnt and used again when children genuinely need to find things out.

Stick Insects

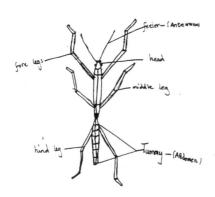

feeler — (Antennae)
fore legs
head
middle leg
hind leg
Tummy — (Abdomen)

a magnified egg

FEMALE

Stick Insects.

Contents.

Glossary.

Abdomen	–	tummy.
antenae	–	feeler.
thorax	–	throat.
moulting	–	shedding skin.
ventral	–	side by the stomach.
laboratory	–	somewhere to do chemistry.
varies	–	to change from one thing to another.
palish	–	not very dark.
productive	–	to produce a lot.
completion	–	to finish.
ceases	–	stops
nymph	–	child insect
nocturnal	–	to come out at night

Stick Insects.

1. **Description.**

The laboratory stick insect varies in colour from shades of green to brown with darker speckles or mottling. Males being very rare. The stick insect cannot see. No hearing organs have been found and the insects have no colour vision. The females can be distinguished from the males by the pink colour of the inner leg.

2. **Habits.**

During the day the stick insects rest with their antennae and the first two pairs of legs are drawn forward, the third pair lying backwards along either side of the abdomen or tummy. In this position they can exactly resemble a twig and lay motionless for hours on end. If they are disturbed they will fall off the twig or cling on with their legs tightly. Stick insects can climb very well, even on a smooth glass surface by means of a pad similar to that of a house fly. They have this pad between the claws on the last joint of each leg.

3. **Life history.**

The females usually begin to lay eggs two or three weeks after their final moult. The eggs are round and about half the size of a match head. They are dark brown with a flat palish yellow cap. Two or three eggs are laid each day but as the female gets older she becomes less productive.

- 2 -

Several hundred eggs may be laid by each female, and after completion of her egg laying, she gradually changes in colour to a dull brown and ceases to feed and eventually dies.

4. **Experiments.**

1. Watch out for egg nymph and adult of the stick insect.
2. The stick insect will grow langer after each moult. If you measure it after it has shedded its skin you will see how much it grows every time it moults. Measure different parts of the body to see if they have grown longer besides the body.
3. If you had a batch of nymphs in a warm place and a batch of nymphs the same age in a cold place, see if there is any change in growth.
4. Collect the stick insects skins because creatures with hard outside skins have to cast their skins as they grow.
5. With a lens it is possible to make out the mouth parts of the stick insects. Watch them eating.
6. The stick insect can protect itself by colour and camouflage. How?
7. Does the colour of the food effect the colour of the stick insect? Try feeding them on ivy as well as privet.

Stick insects pamphlet by Leonie, aged eight

```
                        - 3 -

5.    How to look after stick insects.

      To look after stick insects you would need a cage or an
      old fish tank and a glass jar of water, with some privet
      inside it for the stick insect to eat.  Once every
      three or four days you will have to change the fish tank
      or cage, because they eat a lot of privet.
```

```
                        - 4 -

                    Cross Word.

Across.    1.    Stick ?  (6)
           3.    Another word for feeler  (7)
           5.    How many legs has a stick insect  (3)
           7.    What do you need to put the water in  (3)
           8.    They like Ivy and  ?  (6)
          10.    What is the posh word for stomach or tummy  (7)
          11.    Another word for thorax  (5)
          12.    When it sheds its skin  (8)


Down.      1.    They like to eat privet and  ?  (3)
           2.    What has a palish cap  (3)
           4.    Fish  ?  (4)
           6.    The males are very  ?  (4)
           9.    What is another word for throat  (6)
          11.    Another word for abdomen  (5)
```

Stick insects pamphlet cont.

Leonie visited the school library and her local library to find out more about stick insects. There seemed to be little information available. This forced Leonie to use her existing knowledge about how to find information. She needed the following library skills:
– how are books catalogued?
– where would you expect to find books about stick insects?
– how do you select relevant books?
– can she use an index?
– can an encyclopaedia help?

The children were also asked to visit Central Library since there was so little information available. Leonie arrived back at school with four books, but only one contained a small amount of information.

The teacher also did some research at the local teachers' centre and found a very technical pamphlet specifically about stick insects. The readability level was very difficult, but nevertheless she showed it to the children, explaining that it was written for people studying the creatures in depth. This did not deter Leonie and her friends, who took it away to read. They soon began to check details written in the pamphlet by looking at the insects. Their reading skills were tested here, but, undeterred, they decided to make notes and look up definitions of any scientific or technical language they came across. Having done this they tried to fit the definitions into the sentence. They were trying to make sense of the text and much oral discussion took place. Only when they became really stuck did they check with their teacher. When she discussed their research with them they agreed the text was difficult but said they were enjoying finding things out.

The information began to fascinate them. They began looking for eggs, observing the stick insects' eating habits and spent a great deal of time discussing colour and camouflage, constantly referring to the reference material.

They went to their teacher and suggested it would be a good idea if they could write a pamphlet for other children in school telling them all about stick insects and how to care for them. Leonie decided the pamphlet must contain a glossary since the reference book had one. They realised they needed to read the information they had collected from various sources and disseminate this in a simple form. They needed to remember the audience they had determined for themselves and to keep in mind their aim. During the process of writing the pamphlet it was possible to identify a variety of skills used by the children. They:
- selected relevant information
- kept in mind the glossary
- ordered information into headings/paragraphs
- left out information which seemed irrelevant
- added extras gleaned from first-hand experience
- suggested experiments
- discussed, redrafted, edited
- made decisions
- co-operated and collaborated
- sought opinions
- used note-taking strategies
- re-read the drafts
- considered presentation
- used a scientific/technical genre
- added a sense of fun (crossword)
- kept in mind a sense of audience

The work inspired other children in the class who became interested in the life of the stick insects and suggested further experiments and hypotheses. One very low-attaining pupil, John (aged eight), created his own pamphlet based very much on information he had gleaned by listening to the ongoing class discussions, feedback, and from direct observation.

In conclusion, it can be said that if there is a purpose then reading becomes goal-directed and efficient. Children do possess the ability to select relevant information and appropriate material from a whole range of books. They become skilled at finding their way through books. They are able to select, analyse, summarise, evaluate and reorganise information in the light of first-hand experience.

Case study: Butterflies

This study considers the interactive nature of reading and writing and offers a viewpoint that writing in school is not something separate and divorced from real life. We suggest that reading for information is most meaningful if it arises out of the curriculum and is not always prescribed by the teacher.

Children, we believe, are more motivated when there is a genuine requirement to find something out. Pre-school children learn language without knowing any of the rules. The reason why they learn so readily is because they do so in the course of using it to satisfy their own purposes. We argue that intentions and purposes are the indispensable keys to learning. If children are presented with a reading situation in which they can see little purpose they are unlikely to devote as much energy and attention to the task as they would if they could appreciate that it has a purpose which is directly relevant to them.

There is a danger that we as teachers may have a clear understanding of the purposes of the tasks we set our children, but the child may see no purpose in them at all or may consider that the task is to please the teacher rather than to learn the skill because it is needed for reading. If this is the case, learning will suffer in two ways:

1. motivation to learn will be reduced — learning will become less efficient;
2. the child may not be able to transfer the skills to other situations.

Evidence shows that we, as teachers, do not offer enough opportunities or reasons for writing or reading. We are suggesting that no matter how good the teacher's intentions are, the quality of learning will not be as effective as it would if it was negotiated naturally. As long as the driving force behind the activity remains that of the teacher, children will be deprived of opportunities to explore what they are learning.

We have found that by setting up reading environments that encourage children's development of their own intentions, motivation is greater and reading becomes a purposeful activity. We believe that the children's ability to discover and then implement intentions for reading will emerge gradually as a result of exposure to repeated opportunities for this kind of investigation and a climate of expectations in which the teacher is seen as a trusted adult willing to share in the research process.

This requires much work on the part of the teacher and an understanding of the reading process. We must find the most effective ways to challenge the thinking of children, capitalise on their curiosity, recognise individual differences and encourage intellectual exploration.

The following examples serve to illustrate this sort of approach.

Laura, aged eight, brought a box of butterflies to school because it related to the ongoing area of study in her class. She wanted to identify them, and here we can see a genuine need as well as the fact that Laura's curiosity was aroused. At this point, other friends became involved and collaborative learning was beginning to happen. The children needed to read in order to find out information. Reading was seen as enjoyable, but also satisfying a personal curiosity. The teacher's role was one of helping the children towards an understanding of the strategies needed to cope with the complex task. Laura, therefore, has declared her own purposes for reading. She is able to speculate about the information she seeks using books found at home, in libraries and in school. Laura has consulted books with illustrations about butterflies from abroad and can say which was her favourite book and which was the most useful book. She is able to comment on difficulties she experienced in finding information. Laura is becoming a discerning reader who has met a variety of styles and is able to make judgements about the impact that different books had on her research. With a regular diet of this sort of experience, Laura will learn to make appropriate choices of reading material in relation to her own particular reading purposes and to read the material with deeper insight.

Laura's own reasons for wanting to find out more about her butterflies were threefold:

1. to learn about butterflies
2. because I enjoy it
3. to make a book about moths and butterflies for other people.

If children have a purpose, they go to the text with questions already in mind. One way of sorting this information is in matrix form. They can set themselves questions they wish to have answered and list the butterflies they wish to research. If a box in the grid remains empty then they must seek elsewhere for further information.

Butterflies	Cabbage White	Common Blue	Peace Blossom
Does it fly?			
Does it find a safe place to hibernate?			
Does it live in hot countries?			
Does it lay eggs on leaves?			
Does it die during winter?			

They then need to plan how to present the finished product. Decisions need to be made as to how they are going to use the information gained, which information to reject and what the finished product will look like. Should it be a polished piece of writing, a pamphlet or an annotated picture?

What has been said is aimed at helping children to develop skills as critical readers. Critical readers read to test their assumptions and fulfil their stated purposes. They need to adopt a problem-solving approach to reading by asking relevant questions and being able to process the information and validate answers in the light of their experiences.

This experience in Laura's case was also influenced by her parents. It transpired that the butterflies belonged to Laura's father and she had been told how her father had captured them without hurting them by using 'a special suitcase with a light bulb in' before pinning them.

If comprehension involves the relating of ideas read in the text to ideas already known and integrated into the individual's picture and understanding of the world, then the reader becomes involved in a balancing act while reading. Laura's reading has involved a balancing act between what her family has told her and what she reads in books. Some issues, however, are not dealt with specifically in books. In this case Laura and her friends had to address the question, 'is it right to catch butterflies?' and this led to a class discussion. Laura chose to offer this thoughtful piece of writing:

I think that it is cruel to kill butterflies and moths because they only live for a short time. We wouldn't like it if we were killed and pinned on a piece of wood. They look nice in the open air. I think you should get the ones which are dead already.

My dad caught some in a kind of suitcase that had a light bulb inside and a hole for them to go in. This is how it works. They go in through the hole because they are attracted to the light. Then they drop down and you have caught them.

Laura's reading became goal-directed and efficient because she had a genuine reason to find out some information. She was able to evaluate the material in the light of a first-hand experience − her box of pinned butterflies. The library played a crucial role as the resource centre for her research. This valuable resource must be at the top of our educational objectives and teaching and learning must be geared to it from a very early age.

We have argued that the process as well as the product is meaningful to children, but we must tell them how to cope with the process.

From Laura's experiences, either first-hand or vicarious, she was able to offer this thoughtful comment after her deliberations on the rights and wrongs of catching butterflies:

All this book reading made me wonder if it's OK to kill butterflies.

Case study: I am an ecologist

The following examples illustrate how children can write for different purposes and from differing starting points. Beverley (aged eight) completed a book after work on mini-beasts. The contents page shows the format of the book.

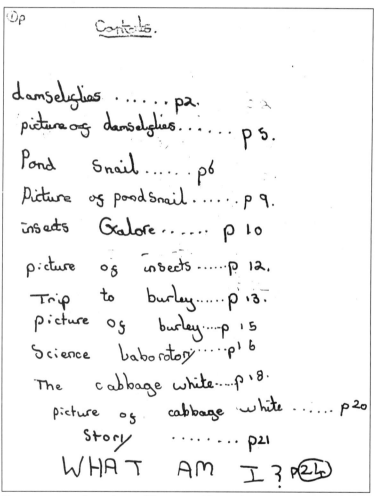

Contents page from damselflies pamphlet by Beverley, aged eight

The topic arose because of work mentioned earlier about stick insects. The children's interest in insects had been aroused and it was agreed to research this further. The work inspired a visit to a pond in the summer term to verify research done in the classroom. We investigated the lifestyle and habitats of a variety of creatures by deciding that it would not be sensible for all the class to choose the same mini-beasts to study. Our research coincided with a TV programme which proved a rich source of information. With the help of television and reference materials found in various libraries, Beverley was able to offer the following information about damselflies.

P1

Damselflies.

Damselflies are like Dragonflies but a smaller version. They both have brightly coloured bodys and their length from the head to the abdomen is 3.5. The damselfly has three parts, the first part of it is the head then in it's head there's the Jaw with compound eyes. Compound eyes are made up of millons of dots that helps them to see They have biting Jaws instead of teeth, It's sucks it prey and stabs them with it's sharp Jaws. The second piece of it body is it's thorax. The thorax is it's throat, it has three pairs of legs as well. It's wing span is about .9cm. It is very humpy so

2

that you can see it's muscles working. When it is a adult it clings not walks. It's muscles work with the wing. The third part is it's abdomen which is a long thin peice made up of organs inside. A special organ which is called reproduction organ. The male and female are different colours, the male blue and the female all sorts of bright colours. When they lay eggs they attach themselves to each other. The female lay them and the male fertilised them. The baby damselfly is called a nymph. And nearly all its life it lives in a pond. It feeds and grows in a pond. The damselfly and the nymph are carnivorous eaters that means their meat eaters. The nymphs

P3

have very good eyesight. The nymphs have feather shaped fins at the rear which act as gills through which the nymphs extract dissolved oxygen out of the water. When it is fully grown it gets on a stalk and sheds it skin and becomes an adult damselfly and carries on life growing and feeding on smaller flys and mates and lays eggs.

P5

A DAMSELFLY.

Damselflies pamphlet by Beverley, aged eight

This was a first attempt, written using notes made during the programme and after discussion with the class. Reference material provided the detail, but most of the writing is original. Beverley's description of a visit to our local Middle School, 'The Science Laboratory', is honest, thoughtful, yet full of detail.

The Science Laboratory.

Friday, 22nd June, We went to a School called St Georges, it was a very big School. Two girls called Samatha and Bernadette met us at the gates and showed us up the stairs and into the science lab. Really it was just like an ordinary class-room apart from all the animals in there. In sort of a fish tank there was some locusts inside. Locusts look a bit like grasshoppers but more colourful. They were some agrican toads. The Toads were very big and these Toads eat worms. They was a green lizard which had a very long tail.

When you watch that lizard closely, you could see its pounch in its throat breathing. They had a snake. It was a grass snake it was very timid. They had three gerbils called chip n dale and cheescake. 3 hamsters called mussels and Noddy and the other had a disease — his name was Henry G. They was a mouse called Timothy. We saw some preserved animals in jars there they were Some crabs and Starfish and Some chicks, a newt, a male Toad baby gerbils, caterpillars a snake. I fed The agrican Toads with a long worm. It was a Super morning.

The Science Laboratory by Beverley, aged eight

She has the audience very much in mind here and is at pains to explain points she feels will help the reader. The experience of handling the creatures or looking carefully exudes from the text. The reader is made to share Beverley's moments with the lizard.

When you watch that lizard closely you could see its pouch in its throat breathing.

Beverley's care and concern for creatures and the environment was enhanced by this topic and their vulnerability became very apparent as she learned more about their lifestyles. Her treatment of cruelty to a spider in a story written after her project underlines her concerns.

. . . Jonathan spotted the old mother spider. He started to squash it but she just got out of the way. She started to slow down and then squash! she was dead. In the morning the little spider looked everywhere for his mother. He found her squashed. Who could do such a thing? cruel, unkind, cold hearted people that's who . . .

and again:

Mister Spider looked for some food and at last found some. Bye fly I'm off on an adventure. I'm just warning you it can be cruel that world.

Beverley wanted to include a quiz in her book and again we can see her concern for living things.

What am I?
I have very long legs and I can run like the wind.
I can't fly which is such a shame
You hunt me for feathers to make feather hats
I'm a bird and I live in Africa.

The work was climaxed by a request from Beverley to choreograph and present her own ballet, 'The spider and the fly'. With a friend she made a spider's web and with parental help found some appropriate music and costumes. She performed her dance as part oi an end-of-term finale which included music, poetry, dance, drama and song, based around the theme of mini-beasts.

Case study: Writing and the design process

The role of design as a central feature of the primary curriculum is now widely recognised as a key factor in moves towards investigative learning. Recent statutory requirements for science and mathematics as part of the National Curriculum have emphasised the investigative and exploratory nature of work whereby children are increasingly given the freedom to investigate problems and find their own solutions. The further development of the National Curriculum with statutory requirements for Design Technology will continue to establish this approach within the primary classroom. The role of language is central to the approach as a means of not only communicating problems and their solutions to others, but also as a means of sharing ideas and suggestions as children journey through the process. The referential form of writing therefore takes on even greater significance as the design process incorporates all three components of the written form as identified by Kinneavy (1971) (see p.40). Exploratory, Informative and Scientific writing are each important areas of the design process as design itself involves the gathering of information and exploring of ideas and indeed the scientific/practical application of theories as designs are developed into prototype models.

This creates the demand for the communication of observations and ideas and consequently the writing of design ideas, instructions and explanations of the design process. Work in the design area of the curriculum particularly creates opportunities for children to evaluate their own writing by posing questions. For example, are the instructions clearly sequenced? How can we prioritise our instructions and directions? etc. Written evaluations of solutions to identified problems may incorporate self-criticism and all provide children with a genuine purpose for true planning and redrafting of their work. If teacher–pupil and pupil–pupil conferences are established to allow for the open, collaborative redrafting of work, then not only are the children themselves given greater control over the editing process, but they also have the opportunities to develop a deeper understanding of the language and its structure.

The writing demands associated with design and problem-solving techniques require a logic and style of their own. Therefore, if true breadth of writing experience is to be fostered and children given the opportunities to develop their thought processes to cope with a variety of higher-level cognitive demands that will be made upon them, it is essential that the opportunities for exploratory, informative and scientific writing that arise in group problem-solving and design activities are seized upon whenever possible.

Squirrel-proof bird feeders

In connection with a topic on Autumn, a visit was made to a local countryside centre. During the visit, the children explored the environment searching for signs of animal life. The grey squirrel featured prominently in the visit and this was extended when back at school. Children found information about the grey squirrel and its habits/lifestyle. As part of the research the children watched a video of a BBC television programme 'Daylight Robbery', introduced by Jessica Holm. In the video, the habits of the grey squirrel and its predilection for taking food left out in domestic gardens for birds are discussed. The video showed experiments in the design of squirrel-proof bird feeders. This stimulated great interest among the children and they too began to experiment with their own designs. Working collaboratively in teams, language became an important features of the process as ideas and suggestions were shared with the group.

Several designs were produced and children were encouraged to explain their designs in writing, sharing their explanations of the complex workings of the design and the way the prototype was to be produced.

Explanations and directions were written by the children to accompany their illustrated design and then shared with a wider audience. Other children were encouraged to question the designers if the written explanations were not clear and together the children began to understand the need for clarity in the explanation of design. Groups of children, working in 'conferences' then discussed the design, its appropriateness to the task and the written instructions and explanations. The group questioned it and made suggestions and constructive criticism of the shared ideas. The conferencing and sharing of suggestions and thoughts among friends was not seen as threatening and was only attempted if the designers wanted to take part. Consequently, suggestions and ideas were received favourably by the children and many of the initial designs were redrafted to incorporate further detail.

When the children were happy with their designs and the clarity of their ideas, prototype models were constructed. Although the completed models were not tested in the environment, controlled experiments were undertaken in the classroom and an evaluation of their practicality and success was made.

The genuine problem

As the design of squirrel-proof bird feeders had been a natural extension of a shared experience by the children, albeit a second-hand one, opportunities should be made for children to solve the problems they themselves have identified, genuine problems that they have experienced first-hand. Throughout the book we have emphasised the importance of children having a genuine purpose to write. Case studies have shown how the genuine purpose has developed from the children themselves and the experiences they have shared. The same applies to design. If the task does not have genuine relevance or meaning to the children involved or is an isolated task that does not relate to the children's direct experience, there may be a lack of real conviction, depth of understanding and genuine involvement on the part of the child.

Ample opportunities do arise where real problems are identified by the children and where the children have a genuine reason for wishing to respond. In such situations, written work not only forms the mode of communication but provides children with a mode of expression and a means of developing their own logic and thought sequence. The following two experiences highlight ways in which problems, identified by the children incidentally, have developed into thought-provoking and well-organised design work maintaining relevance and meaning to the designers involved.

Coastal erosion

During a visit to the coast with a class of seven- to eight-year-old children, a section of the cliff that had recently collapsed into the sea, closing the coastal path at that point, provided an ideal introduction to problems created by coastal erosion. The children wanted to know why the cliff had collapsed and the situation prompted a discussion about the reasons for erosion. On returning to school, a simulation tank was constructed and the children, using a variety of natural materials including clay, soil, sand and stone, reconstructed a series of headlands and bays similar to those seen at the coast. Water was introduced into the tank and waves were made to simulate those seen at the coast. Before very long the sand started to shift and the clay section of the cliff began to subside and fall into the water.

The problem of cliff erosion was genuine. Children had experienced it first-hand. They were able to observe the reasons for the erosion and had the opportunity to tackle the problem themselves. It was genuine, it was relevant and had grown from their direct experience.

Groups of children set about designing, constructing and testing their own anti-erosion devices. Explanations were written, instructions for their mass production were sequenced, and the genuine problem-solving activity elicited a wealth of writing activity.

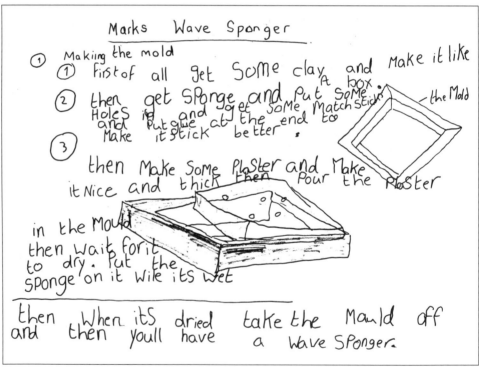

Mark's wave sponger by Mark, aged eight

Understanding the solar system

As part of the school organisation, five classes of seven- to nine-year-old children were split into ten smaller teaching groups twice per week for practical science, maths and design problem-solving activities to complement work taking place in the classroom. The ten smaller mixed-ability groups were named after the nine planets and the sun present in our solar system and were to be rotated each half term. During preparation work at the beginning of the year, children researched the solar system

To Make our solar system.

First you need some wood some string and some plasticene. you need to cut a long piece of wood for the top which the planets turn round on. this has to stick on to a thin round stick like a pencil. the string is wrapped round the round stick and there is a stand at the

bottom. make the planets out of plasticene in the right order and hang them from the long piece of wood. Then we pull the long string. the sun will turn around and the wood which the planets are on will stick to the sun so when the sun turns around the long round wood will turn round aswell. The wood stand will stop the pencil wood stick

from falling over. when the wood arm turns round the planets will rotate around the sun.

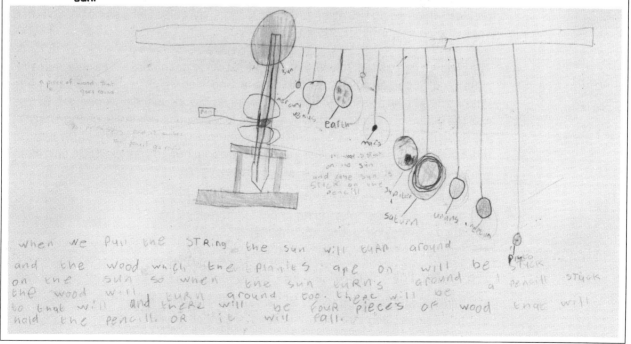

To make our solar system by Shabana, aged eight

and specific planets within it. Following research, children were encouraged to make models of the solar system to reinforce their knowledge about it. During the making of these models, several children approached the problem of how to rotate their model. The children themselves had identified the problem and therefore the teacher encouraged the children to design ways of overcoming it. Different power sources were experimented with, different rotation systems were observed in action and the children set about making their own designs. Children talked their way through the workings of their designs and were encouraged to write this down. The models were then constructed by groups of children using the designs and written explanations and the children's problem-solving process reached a number of satisfying conclusions, each design and completed model being individual in character but equally successful in answering the problem which the children had set out to overcome.

Case study: Designing a theme park

We had the opportunity to take forty five- to six-year-olds to a local resource centre which aims to promote INSET on design technology on one morning a week for ten weeks. The timing of our visit coincided with the publication of the Secretary of State's proposals for design and technology (DES/WO 1989c).

We wanted to create a meaningful situation for the children and, at the same time, develop our own monitoring and evaluation programme for recognising achievement. As with all our case studies we felt the emphasis should be placed on the learning process. The aim of our proposals for design and technology, in line with National Curriculum recommendations, was to stimulate originality, the practical capability in designing and making, and to build on existing good practice, which sees problem solving as an opportunity for both teachers and children to enter into a spirit of enquiry. The project forced different styles of teaching and learning to be established since the children were working outside the normal classroom environment and with many more adults than usual.

Our first consideration was to define the problem. We wanted to present a genuine problem which would lend itself to design technology whilst at the same time offering access to cross-curricular opportunities.

The children had visited St Ives, a municipal resource encompassing a café, mansion house, golf course, adventure playground and woodland, with the Countryside Warden during the previous year as part of ongoing work on the environment. St Ives was the centre of a major controversy as the local council wanted to change its use. We thought it would be a good idea to revisit the site with the Countryside Warden in order that the children might offer suggestions about how to improve it. On our return we shared our thoughts and four issues arose:

1. the café was unattractive and needed improving;
2. the mansion was delapidated and needed renovating;
3. the park was uninspiring and unsafe;
4. the golf course held no attraction to the children.

The children finally decided that they would like to:

a) improve and redesign the cafe;
b) make an exciting theme park instead of the golf course.

This decision raised many environmental and recreational issues and the Countryside Warden shared his concerns about what this project would do to the wildlife living there. Since many pressure groups were presenting their case to the local council, we felt our five- to six-year-olds should have the same opportunity. We invited the Councillor at the centre of the controversy to come to school and talk with the children. This he did, leaving them with the task of designing their theme park and café for his attention.

We had our 'real' situation and it was decided to concentrate on improving the café, using ideas generated in the role play corner in the classroom. The theme park would be created at the centre.

Since everyone involved believed that the working environment is a very important element in successful problem solving and the place in which children learn most effectively and develop positive attitudes to learning as well as skills and concepts, a 'helping atmosphere' was defined. We all aimed to offer security to the children to try out new ideas, listen to and discuss any problems that arose and develop positive attitudes in all the children, irrespective of gender or ability. Our role changed from that of provider of information to that of 'question asker' and 'resource provider'. We became observers, occasionally guides, reminding children with the help of a useful question of successful strategies that had helped them resolve previous problems.

We began with a problem – 'how can we build a bridge to carry a mouse across a pond to an island' – in order to highlight the design process. The children constructed bridges from all kinds of materials and at the same time came to know the centre staff.

The following week work on the theme park began. The children were asked to brainstorm the sort of rides they might like to see in their park. They then chose which ride they wanted to make and groups with three or four children were created. They were asked to design their model on paper and make a prototype. This took about four weeks and brought to the fore many skills and concepts the children did or did not possess. We, as staff, videoed, photographed and interviewed the children to try to gain a deeper understanding of the strategies they were using. The work addressed all four attainment targets, identifying needs and opportunities, generating a design proposal, planning and making and appraising. The role of design and technology and its special relationship with maths and science is acknowledged, but for the purpose of this study it would be useful to examine the language potential of the project.

One aspect of the teacher's role that became crucial to this experience was the stimulation of discussion. Discussion plays a vital part in problem solving. Children had to experience for themselves that talking did not only mean comparing solutions or helping each other out, but rather it was needed to solve problems. To begin with the children tended to work alongside each other, but as the project progressed they collaborated and true sharing of ideas began to develop. Talk was used more for negotiation and explanation than for merely answering questions.

When the prototypes were completed the children presented them, explaining any difficulties that had arisen and any intentions they had for improving their finished models. The children were interviewed and a transcript made of what they said. Excerpts from this were printed and displayed next to the models in order for each group to have access to what was happening in general. As the project progressed, opportunities for using the word processor arose as the children were asked to create systems and rules for their rides. The children had visited a fair and discussion had taken place after the visit about issues relating to health and safety, economic awareness and systems. This helped them to produce this safety notice for the see-saw.

Safety notice for a see-saw

They also made posters to advertise their rides and worked out costings.

As the weeks passed, the models began to take shape and technical problems were solved with the help of much discussion with trusted adults. Co-operation improved and the desire to make the models aesthetically pleasing was uppermost in most of the children's minds as this photograph of the water slide illustrates.

The water slide

The roundabout group became heavily involved in solving the problem of how to make it go round. They investigated using marbles as a mechanism for turning but, with a little guidance, solved the problem by using plastic tubes. They decided it should have four swings, each fitted with a safety bar. They solved the problem of reaching the swings by making a portable set of steps. Once the roundabout was finished, the children used the technology to write their description and rules for using it, created a back cloth against which they could photograph their model for future advertising purposes and demonstrated that it did move.

The roundabout

We were concerned that the children should record their achievements in a variety of ways and it was decided that they should choose four things they felt they did well and stick them on a certificate (p.136). They then had to choose one thing they liked about their model. This was done on a one-to-one basis with a teacher. The children then discussed their certificates with each other.

The finale resulted in a presentation of their models to the staff at the centre, and of course, each other. The models produced were a see-saw, ghost train, roller coaster, bumper cars, waterslide, hang-glider swing, roundabout, dragon train and swings. The children displayed evidence of a sense of pride in their achievements, a confidence to present their models, enthusiasm and excitement and an understanding of the processes they had encountered.

Of course, we could not end the project without inviting Councillor Farley back. He duly responded to the invitation and made the children's presentation a two-way process by asking very genuine questions. He promised to listen to the children's criticisms and constructive comments and keep them informed of further happenings.

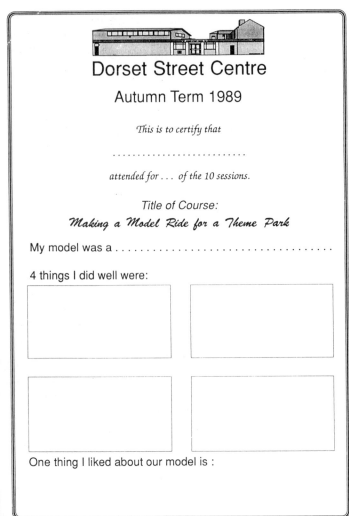

Certificate of Achievement

If the inclusion of design and technology as a foundation subject in the National Curriculum is 'a recognition that the capability to investigate, design, make and appraise is as important as the acquisition of knowledge' and that this will not only benefit our children personally but 'will also be an essential condition for the future prosperity of our business and industry', then projects such as this with children so young can only be of benefit.

Hesitancy and dependency in children is replaced by enthusiasm and confidence to tackle different situations . . . If the emphasis is on the process as opposed to the outcome, then there can be no wrong answers, only different routes, and the fear of failure is diminished.

Historical writing

One area of the curriculum often said to be neglected in the primary phase is that of history. The proposals for the teaching of history in the National Curriculum set out by the Secretary of State seek to redress the balance (DES/WO 1990). We are told of 'the need to renew faith in history as a subject for study in schools' (p.3, para. 1.27) and of the Secretary of State's concerns about the quality of history teaching.

Taken as a whole, school history in England and Wales is varied in quality, quantity and organisation. <u>All</u> pupils should receive the best possible teaching in history and much less needs to be left to chance than has recently too often been the case.

(ibid. p.2, para 1.3)

Through the National Curriculum, the Secretary of State has declared a need 'to effect certain improvements'. The following statements underline his intention to ensure history is given an important place in the curriculum.

i)   to achieve a minimum common base of school history for all pupils;
ii) to fortify the position of history in primary schools.

(ibid. p.3, para 1.27)

The aims of the teaching of history are to inform about the present, to teach for an understanding of change and evidence, and, very importantly, to develop the imagination. Key concepts, those of evidence, change and time can be developed in many cross-curricular ways, but never in an isolated context. The concept of evidence is as fundamental to the historian as experiment is to the scientist. Evidence can take many forms: something written, a map, a building, artefacts or memories still alive. The linguistic potential in the search for evidence is enormous. Children need to develop critical questioning approaches to historical knowledge. Teachers should seize on the fact that the search for evidence can create problem-solving activities. Young children should be encouraged to construct narratives from evidence, and the use of eyewitness accounts or visits to places of interest or museums provide exciting stimuli. Skills children will be using in relation to written sources will be reading, comprehension, library skills and communication.

The following case studies describe how, using an historical stimulus, writing emerged in a variety of genres, showing a rich use of language and emotions.

Case study: Settle to Carlisle Railway

Learning about the history of the railway was to form the central theme of an extended visit to a Youth Hostel in Stainforth. The aim was to get the children to empathise with the people who built it with the help of visual and descriptive materials. In preparation for the visit, the children analysed reference materials about the construction of the railway, learnt songs which told its story, and explored photographs of the shanty towns and artefacts used by the navvies. In order to truly empathise with the conditions and lifestyle the men and women endured whilst building the railway we visited the site.

It was a snowy February weekend when we arrived and although the children were well researched no amount of secondary information could take the place of that direct experience. The vastness of the viaduct overawed the children as did the thought of working on it without the comforts of a modern-day existence. They dug up evidence of pottery still buried in the shanty town and experienced the extreme cold the navvies would have had to endure. We visited the local church and the children were able to find more information from the gravestones. The direct experience enabled them to assess the value of the stories and songs they had heard and to evaluate the written and photographic sources they had already researched. The visit encouraged a disciplined use of the imagination and raised awareness as to 'our and theirs', of who

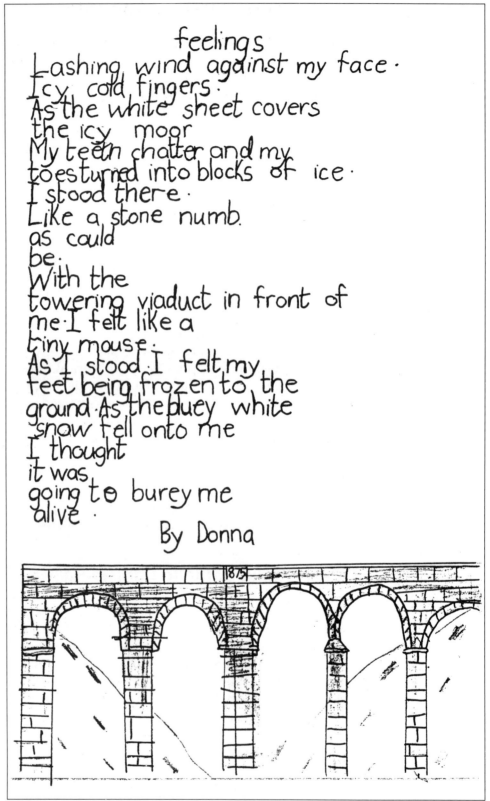

Feelings by Donna, aged eight

we are and our place in time. It enabled them to better understand 'our' inheritance, and coincided with the national protests being made to save the Settle to Carlisle Railway. Above all, the project encouraged an evermore complex development of thought and language through listening, speaking and writing. Donna's poem (above) conveys her feelings as she stood beneath the viaduct.

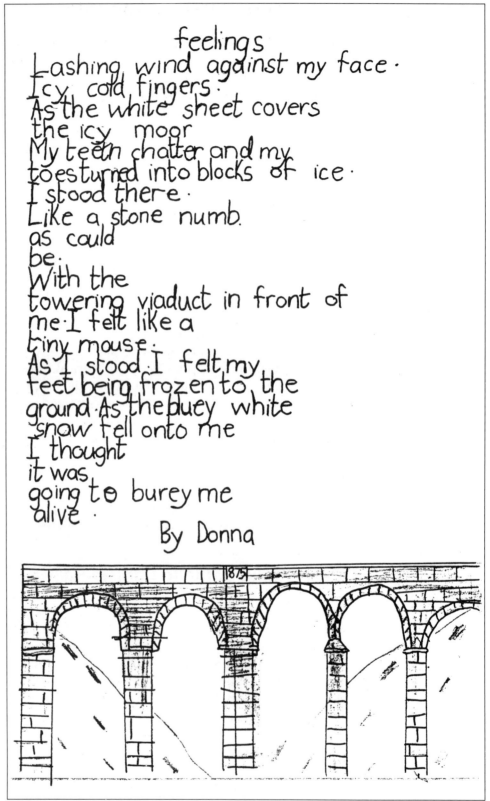

Case study: A visit to Clarke Hall

Museum artefacts and old houses offer an excellent stimulus for historical investigations. Such a resource is Clarke Hall, a seventeenth-century house, where children can enjoy a variety of experiences. The staff told us that teachers value Clarke Hall primarily as a seventeenth-century historical project visit. Evaluations done after visits, however, revealed that teachers assessed the value in a great many other ways, and in particular in terms of language development. (See Stevens 1987 for a full discussion of using the Museum as a resource for schools.) We have used the Hall for different reasons, always in role, but to enhance cross-curricular learning.

One group sought refuge whilst fleeing from the Plague. The potential that this work offered in so many areas of the curriculum was enormous.

Such a visit can provide opportunities for children to examine closely primary sources such as objects, furniture, cooking utensils, whole rooms etc. within their historical context and compare and contrast these with present-day examples. We wanted children to examine materials used in the seventeenth century and compare them with modern-day equipment. In costume, we arrived at the house, the children hoping that Mistress Priscilla would let us examine it since we had researched that it was built in the seventeenth century. She agreed to this request, but asked if the children would be prepared to carry out certain tasks in return for her time as she had to prepare the house for very important guests. After a tour of the house in role, during which time she pointed out a wealth of different materials and implements, it was time to break our fast. Writing by Belinda and Claire (both aged eight) shows how they had internalised the correct terminology and which part of their day they chose to describe.

The visit to Clarke Hall

We got dressed in the classroom. We put on a black skirt and a black waistcoat. We wore white socks and black shoes. We wore a collar and a cap and a pinny, so that we could feel what the seventeenth century was like. We had a good time. We got some milk and some parkin to break our fast. We liked the kitchen and we liked the dining room and the bedroom. The kitchen table was so big that thirty-two children were able to eat our lunch at the same time. We had pippins and oranges and some nuts. We had some chicken and pig flesh. We had some colewort and some beetroot and we had some white meat. There was some water to drink. There were some raisins and some bread. In the dining room there were patterns on the ceiling like we've never seen before. They were made with plaster from Paris. We liked roping the bed in the bedroom. Then we went to sit upstairs and Mistress Priscilla told us a story about her friend.

Belinda and Claire aged 8

The visit to Clarke Hall by Belinda and Claire, aged eight

Work on materials combined the disciplines of science and history and the children were engaged in sensory exploration, discussion and analysis, and remembering, comparing and synthesising. Specific activities there included inkmaking, polishing, making an inventory, roping the bed, dyeing wool and cooking.

Back in school, it was decided to make a tape/slide presentation for a parents' evening, using slides taken on the day. The aim of this was to further reinforce learning experienced at Clarke Hall as well as to extend the children's awareness of life beyond their own local environment. The transcript on the opposite page explains the range of activities enjoyed and illustrates evidence of some of the learning that took place.

The science potential in such a visit is enormous in terms of work that can be done investigating materials, heating, lighting, polishing, cooking, writing and examining machinery. One group chose to explore the use of candles at Clarke Hall and carried out a variety of investigations.

The following experiment uses a candle to carry out a fair test when investigating the flame resistance of materials. Emma's writing (aged eight) explains the experiment, and the matrix and the summary were her way of presenting scientific data (p.142).

The teaching of history will fail if we do not seize every opportunity to develop the use of the imagination. Diane (aged nine), wrote the poem on p.143 because she was inspired by work on candles, and it formed the front cover of a book she made about her visit.

The work from Clarke Hall spanned a term and involved much research using reference materials. Paul Noble (1985, p.11) argues for the need to teach history. In quoting the Primary Survey he makes reference to the fact that in eighty per cent of classes which study history the work was superficial.

In many cases it involved little more than copying from reference books and often the theme chosen had very little historical content.

The survey (DES/WO 1978) points to the very large amount of second-hand stimuli being used in the teaching of history, for example television, work cards or story. The authors are also critical of the fact that:

it was rare to find classes where the work, even in a simple way, was leading the children towards an understanding of historical change and the causal factors involved, or where children were becoming aware of the nature of historical evidence.

(ibid., p.73)

Their concern is highlighted further when they tell us:

A factor contributing to this situation has undoubtedly been a lack of planning in the work. Few schools had schemes of work in history, or teachers who were responsible for the planning and implementation of work in this field. While it is true that an appreciation of the perspectives of time develops only slowly in children, it is liable to remain rudimentary unless a coherent approach to helping children acquire an understanding of the past is adopted.

(ibid.)

We went into the bed chamber and saw a four poster bed. Mistress Priscilla asked us to tell her what this was. We had a few guesses then she showed us what to do with it. It was used to warm the bed.

I had to help prepare our meal in the kitchen. I stared into the fire . . . I was staring into the fire because it reminded me of Guy Fawkes. It reminded me of bonfire night when all the fires were lit. I felt sad because I thought of witches. The chicken was cooking on the spit. They got the word spit from watching the spit go round and all the fat spitting off it.

This is me dyeing wool. We squashed the ingredients to make the dyes in a pestle and mortar. The wool changed different colours from peach to orange and dark green. It was really hot work.

We played musical instruments. Some made low noises some made high noises. I was playing a racket. It made a noise like a ship wanting to go under a bridge and it goes up slowly. Lee had a big recorder and it made a whistle. There were some instruments like walking sticks and Gail was playing one and so was Gemma. I have forgotten what noise they made. They had a big curved instrument. It was called a cornet. It was leather and it was like a flute. It has holes in it and Gareth is playing it.

Extracts from the children's tape/slide presentation following the trip to Clarke Hall

We got a candle and put it in some sand and Miss Marshall lit the candle and Miss Marshall put on the top of the candle a material and we wrote about the materials and we wrote about the smells. I made a matrix of the results and typed them.

1. Viscose
Did it burn with a flame ?
Yes it did.
It smells like burnt toast.
What does it look like after ?
Black ash.

2. Plastic.
It did not burn with a flame.
It smells of chemicals. It had a hole in it.
It was thin and had been stretched.

3. Paper.
It did not burn with a flame.
It smelt of chocolate.
It was black and sooty.

4. Cotton.
Yes it burned with a flame.
It smelt like a bonfire.
It left a hole with black ash.

5. Wool.
It did not burn with a flame.
It smelt like burned food.
It was black and crumbled when you touched it.

6. Hessian.
It did not burn with a flame.
It smelt like a bonfire .
It left a dark patch.

We think that hessian would be the best thing to wear if you work with fire. It did not burn as easily as the others.

Name of material	How long was it held over flame	Did it burn with a Flame?	What did it Smell like?	What did it look like after.?
1 Viscose	5 Seconds	yes	Burnt toast	Black ash
2 Plastic	5 Seconds	No	chemicals	thin and stretchy
3 Paper	5 Seconds	No	chocolate	Black patch
4 cotton	5 Seconds	yes	firework	hole and burnt at the edges
5 Wool	5 Seconds	No	burnt food	brown and crumbly
6 Hessian	5 Seconds	No	Bonfire	dark patch.

Writing about scientific findings by Emma, aged eight

Candle

Smokey flame make everything shiver
Dull colours
Black wick smoking well
yellow flame burning brightley
Gray smoke like on a rainy day
flame tall looking around
Liquid wax like a river
wax running solid
in candle stick on the table

Candle by Diane, aged nine

The project at Clarke Hall and the work around the Settle to Carlisle railway presented direct experiences which, although cross-curricular in nature, did address the teaching of history. One of our aims was to deal with the dimension of time and it is said that history is the only subject which deals with this. We agree with Paul Noble (ibid., p.7) when he tells us:

An understanding of time past is essential if we are to appreciate fully how today's world grew out of yesterday's. We cannot understand fully our place in the living world unless our knowledge of people and events extends into the dimension of time.

We believe that an examination of utensils and materials past and present and an attempt to empathise with people from the past does help to foster historical understanding.

Conclusion

Teachers have an advantage which is greater than anything educational research has to offer, and that is knowledge of the child. If we know children well, we are in a better position to offer them deeper understanding and make wider reflections about their personal growth. If, as teachers, we can create secure climates in which children can feel confident that what they write will be favourably received and that the teacher is not acting in the role of examiner, then they are more likely to experiment with their writing.

As we have seen, the teacher cannot remain passive. The role of the teacher must be one of facilitator, guiding children through the process of writing. There is a danger, however, that we may be tempted to structure the *content* of children's writing. Since we believe that children's writing is personal, imaginative and creative, it seems inappropriate to structure the content too tightly. Each mode of writing has its own framework and outline structure that children must identify and emulate if they are to exhibit clarity of understanding and style in their writing. The structure of story is well defined as is the structure of debate. It is essential that children are introduced to these frameworks since once they understand the elements of the writing modes and the processes involved, they are free to concentrate on creating their own content. Writing can be likened to driving a car. Once you understand the process involved you are free to concentrate on the road ahead. If we can extend the metaphor a little further, just as it helps to have an idea of the mechanics of the car, writing can be vastly improved by a sound knowledge of the mechanics of language. Language needs to be intelligible to other people, the child as author must keep in mind the reader and basic to all good writing is the need to make someone understand. Writing is indeed a communication of thoughts and ideas and, as such, has a central role in the National Curriculum.

As well as being a facilitator, we feel that the teacher's role must be one of motivator. We have suggested that the teacher's skill in motivating pupils is far more important than the particular teaching style or the stimulus presented. Our thoughts are endorsed by Yamamoto (1972) whose very telling pronunciation leaves us in no doubt as to the importance of motivation.

Relative to achievement, motivation is perhaps even more complex and more significant than intelligence itself. Without adequate motivation the intelligent child is hardly a match for his less intelligent but highly motivated peer. A significant factor in motivation is anticipated success – the feeling that the task in hand can be completed . . . the child's concept of ability may be as crucial to his success as his ability *per se.*

We have found that the children with the highest IQs do not necessarily produce the best writing, but in order to arrive at this conclusion it is necessary to look beyond the problems of spelling and grammar and examine the author's intentions.

From our research, we have found that the stimulus for writing is not always the key factor in determining quality. We have argued for the value of the first-hand experience of the tasks we set and for the value of allowing and indeed encouraging children to make up their own titles and negotiate their own writing tasks. We would like to pose the following two questions.

- Is there a threshold beyond which children do not need a stimulus?
- Is there a point in their cognitive and affective development at which they feel secure enough to follow their own volitions?

There is still a great deal of research to be undertaken and indeed we are only at the beginning as regards understanding the writer and the writing process. In this book we have attempted to highlight current research in the field of writing and the importance of providing children with opportunities to write for a broad range of writing purposes and in a broad range of styles. It is only through this that a child can develop as a true writer, adapting styles and forms to suit both the purpose of the task and the audience involved. Our underlying message to teachers is much deeper than this, however. It asks teachers to think carefully about the reasons children are asked to write.

- Is the task relevant or meaningful to every child?
- What are we actually asking of children?
- Are we genuinely wanting the children's views and feelings or are we wanting them to write what the teacher wants to hear?

Our view is that writing tasks given to children need to be genuine and have a real purpose behind them, but successful writing is more to do with the environment and teacher–pupil relationship than the task itself. Where an atmosphere exists that encourages children to write and express themselves in the knowledge that *every* child's work and contribution will be valued on individual terms and not compared with some standard norm, then real writers can develop in the knowledge that they may experiment and grow in confidence within a secure and trusting environment. If a child entering the journey of writing is given the opportunity to develop his or her writing skills

```
          THE CANAL


          The trees curve over the canal,
          There's a shoal of fish swimming along.
          Mayflies fly through the air
          Then disappear in despair.
          It was from a fish
          Down, down deep.
          Then the fisherman gets a trout,
          The one that ate the mayfly.
          A catfish swam gently down the canal.
          Down, down deep.
          Then the fisherman caught a catfish,
          The same one,
          Down, down deep.
```

The Canal by Duncan, aged seven

From a Winter Forest to a Summer Garden.

James sat in his large armchair looking at the photographs of his Grandchildren who were coming to stay for the Christmas holidays.

"I wonder if Michael and William will find the big garden?" he thought, "I shan't tell them where it is."

The train pulled in at the last station on the journey and 'Windermere Station' was cried by the porter on the platform. William looked out of the window of the carriage.

"Just look at those mountains," exclaimed William, "they're as high as the Alps!"

Michael looked at William, "not that big," he said, seriously.

They jumped off the train and made their way across the platform to a man beckoning from a motor car.

"Master Michael," he called, "Master William, tha' Grandad will be waiting for thee. Your trains half an hour late in." Billy Leathwaite, a farmers son, who sometimes drove motor cars for extra money, looked quite annoyed and opened the back door for the boys without a word and did not utter another word until they reached the lakeside road.

"Gosh that lake must be the size of the Pacific!" gasped William. Michael didn't comment but spluttered rather loudly.

"Tha' Grandad lives right on the shore, 'is own boat-house and everything," said Billy, and the boys saw him smile for the first time.

They drove on past a steamer pier where a village was developing and quite soon the road looped away from the lake shore. Shortly they were curving back in and Billy pulled up outside quite a large grey house.

"Here you are, Belle House, tha' Grandads house." Michael and William climbed out and said "thankyou" to Billy. They looked about them. On the right-hand side of the road were steep forested slopes, on the left was the house. It seemed shrouded in dark

From a Winter Forest to a Summer Garden by Duncan, aged fourteen

within this secure, encouraging environment and his or her writing experience is not only varied but has genuine reason and purpose, then if you observe that child writing at seven (p.145) and again at fourteen years of age (above) you will see the increasing depth, quality and style that are the distinguishing features of the emergent author.

woods also. They walked along the short drive and rapped on the door. The door opened and Michael and William saw their Grandad for the first time they could remember.

"Oh, well, how you've grown" said James.

This was too much for the scientific Michael, "I would have thought it was logical that we've grown, folk usually do." Michael thought this very clever, but obviously James was cleverer.

"Ah, but I never said, 'you've grown,'" said James, "but I said, 'how you've grown' meaning you've grown more than I expected, I wouldn't be surprised in the least that you'd grown."

There was nothing Michael could do but leave it at that.

From a Winter Forest to a Summer Garden cont.

Appendix: Children's storywriting

A response framework for evaluating stories written by eight- to nine-year-old children

1. Character: introductory notes

Perhaps the most important element in the stories children write is that of character. We feel that an understanding of the following points is necessary if we are to consider fully the author's skill in his or her use of characterisation.

Firstly, the way in which the author chooses to introduce characters will obviously affect the quality and the logic of the story. The author must therefore take care in choosing the best method of revelation for his or her particular story if use of characterisation is to enhance its quality. In your opinion, has the author's chosen method contributed to the effectiveness of the story?

Secondly, just as in real life people have living relationships with each other, so in story characters must also 'live' in order that the reader might respond to the various ways in which characters develop and interact. In judging the quality of the author's skill in presenting character relationships a number of questions must be considered. If there is evidence of particular relationships, for example, a struggle or deep friendship, is this particular feeling justified within the context of the story? Does the author make the relationships explicit or are they implicit within the story? Whichever device the author has chosen, is it possible to state whether the story has been enhanced by his or her treatment of characterisation?

The way in which characters behave should be consistent with their age and background within the context of the story. As children of eight to nine years follow similar developmental patterns in their personal growth, much of this experience will be reflected in their writing. For example, the expression of humour follows certain developmental stages, as of course does moral and cognitive reasoning. We should look, therefore, for any indication to suggest that the author is demonstrating a particular stage of his or her development through storywriting.

Much has been said and written which would suggest that children as authors do express their own personal concerns and feelings in story and these are usually reflected through use of characterisation. Perhaps the vital question to ask here is: to what degree does the author express this or her own personal concerns and what effect does this have on the story as a whole?

Authors often write themselves into their stories. Is there any evidence that the author as character has depicted in the story events he or she has actually experienced, either first-hand, or vicariously? Does the author offer a factual recounting of experience or has he or she attempted to invent characters in order to produce a fantasy story?

Character speaks to us as readers because we recognise that we too have experienced similar feelings. Has the author been successful in creating characters who fulfil this function? Character also determines incident. How successful has the author's use of characterisation been in contributing to the vitality of the story as a whole?

2. Plot

Basically, when considering plots in the stories children write we are concerned with what is happening. If the author has been successful, then his or her writing will tell a good story and arouse our expectations. Several skills are needed in handling plots and we need to look for such points as whether the story is told in a logical sequence, if the plot is well constructed, and whether the author has been successful in relating prior events to present occurrences.

Children are attempting to make sense of the world and exactly how successful they have been can often be detected from their ability to use language in order to draw observations together and construct cognitive hypotheses in an attempt to solve the problems which they as authors have made for themselves within the context of the story.

Television, literature and personal experiences provide much stimulus for imaginative play, cognitive and affective development, but possibly the most successful storywriter is the author who avoids merely retelling the stimulus and who seeks to develop the ideas provided by the stimulus in order to construct the plot. We should consider, therefore, how successful the author is in attempting to paint a picture of imagined experience from his or her vision and knowledge of real experience.

As with characterisation, children may use the plot in order to express their concern for how they would like things to be. In other words, the plot or theme may reflect examples of universality of experience, for example, a need for security or a journey. Occasionally, the reader is able to detect one central concern running through the story which would indicate the author's attempt to write about a personal experience. If such evidence exists, does it enhance the story or detract from its effectiveness?

Children enjoy reshaping the world in their 'heads' and making it as they would want it to be. We could then look for any evidence to suggest that the author has shown pleasure in creating a setting that he or she would like to be part of – or alternatively, is there any evidence to suggest that the sheer vividness of a personal experience has been written into the story?

Is the story content tied to the particular setting the author has created, or does the story transcend the setting and have universal implications? If so, has this improved the quality of the story?

3. Setting

Setting is the place, or a series of places, in which the characters interact with each other, with objects or animals during a given period of time. Obviously, the author needs to display his or her skill in certain areas when considering setting. Setting must either remain constant or change locality if the sequence of events so demands whilst at the same time remaining consistent with the plot. Time is an important factor when considering setting and this too must remain consistent with the setting. Time is the ordering of incidents in such a way that the significance of their relationships is apparent. A successful story will depend on how well the author has set the scene, whether in the past, present or future and maintained appropriate consistencies between time and setting, and plot and setting.

Setting may be either incidental to the story theme or it may dominate the story. If setting does dominate the story, has the author been successful in creating the appropriate mood? Does the mood of the story direct the reader's response ensuring a feeling of satisfaction after having read the story? Successful setting will show evidence of the author's display of sensitivity to the demands of his or her environment. Is the story enhanced by strongly visual descriptions or the author's keen eye for detail? Is the author consistent in the quality of the care taken to describe each piece of setting as the story unfolds?

Settings may be real or imaginary, not both. Is it possible to decide whether the settings occur in real life or in an imaginary world? If the author has attempted to portray either a fantasy or imaginary setting, how successful has s/he been in projecting his or her imagination into this 'other world'? Has the author been able to handle the limits of the story world perhaps by clearly defining his or her intentions about setting?

4. Style

As children have been asked to produce storywriting as opposed to other forms of writing, any discussion of style must firstly consider whether the writing is an effective story. Such considerations as story beginnings and endings, as well as the author's handling of the various elements discussed above, will contribute to the overall impression of the effectiveness of the story.

The author's communicative strategies – for example, use of subjective narrative or first/third person conventions – will have implications for the overall success of the style of writing and thought needs to be given to these areas when commenting on effectiveness. As we are concerned with children's personal writing, we feel that greater credit should be given if there is evidence to suggest that the language and meaning are the author's own constructs and not handed over by the teacher. Comparison with other stories in the group should help to determine originality of content and ideas.

We are concerned both with the precision and accuracy of linguistic strategies, as well as with the actual story content in terms of ideas and feelings. When evaluating the stories, however, we feel that if a child has adequate control of such areas as spelling, punctuation and structure, then the end-product must be much more acceptable and must affect favourably the overall impression the story makes on the reader. We should consider the language which the author has chosen, in an expressive form, in order to convey ideas, thoughts and feelings for its appropriateness and effectiveness.

Writing is enhanced by sensory images. Is there any evidence which suggests that the author, in his or her use of language, has conveyed a sense of 'felt life' in the story? Does the author achieve this effect by employing any larger scale characteristics in the writing – for example, simile, metaphor, connotation? In other words, we are considering whether or not the author has been successful in using literary devices or stylistic structures in order to convey the story's mood. For example, a letter in a story may indicate the mood of realism, whereas a monster being brought to life by drinking a magic potion suggests a fanciful world.

Children vary in their willingness to be adventurous when using language. To deviate from accepted linguistic conventions and still be successful requires skill and courage on their part. Is there any evidence to suggest that the author has successfully displayed originality and inventiveness in his or her use of language?

Many of the children's stories contain dialogue and we feel this relationship between the story participants can best be discussed under the heading of style of discourse. Adequate control of an appropriate style by the author will naturally lead to a more acceptable piece of storywriting, as well as offering an indication of the child's view of the world, either in realistic terms, or in his or her attempt to produce imaginative writing. The four sets of polarities of style proposed by Leech (1966) seem to be an appropriate model for examining relationships between story participants, particularly the dialogue. A 'colloquial' style is characterised by the presence of idioms, contractions and imperatives, whereas 'formal' style displays a lack of colloquial language. The second set of polarities, 'casual–ceremonial' can best be described by examples of indicators to look for in the text. Such indicators of a 'casual' style are the presence of intimate forms of address, and the use of conversational language contrasted with the more polite forms of address, and requests in deference to demands, which characterise 'ceremonial' style. A third pair of contrasting styles is termed 'personal–impersonal', the former characterised by use of first and second person pronouns and the use of imperatives in a personal style, whereas the latter category shows a marked absence of such pronouns, but a strong presence of third person forms in order to avoid reference to the author, as well as frequent use of the passive voice. The final pair of categories of style on this continuum are termed 'simple–complex'. Indicators in the text of a 'complex' style include such considerations as number of words per sentence and number of main or subordinate clauses per sentence.

As well as being concerned with form, attention ought also to be directed to function, that is whether the child is able to deal effectively with different uses of languages. Is there any evidence to suggest that the author has attempted to use language for different purposes? Is the story enhanced by the author's ability to employ this strategy?

Response framework

1.0 CHARACTER

1.1 *CHARACTERS REVEALED*
How does the author reveal characters?
a) through action
b) through appearance
c) through narration
d) in conversation
e) by naming
f) by the thoughts of others
g) or how?

1.2 *CHARACTER RELATIONSHIPS*
Is there any evidence to suggest any of the following character relationships?
a) a tension
b) a struggle
c) affection
d) friendship
e) bitterness
f) hatred
g) or what?

1.3 *CHARACTER BEHAVIOUR*
Does the author as character express any of the following examples of behaviour?
a) exaggeration
b) incongruity
c) surprise
d) slapstick humour
e) verbal humour
f) moral reasoning
g) compassion
h) decline in egocentricity
i) strength
j) weakness
k) or what?

1.4 *CHARACTERS' PERSONAL CONCERNS*
Does the author as character express:
a) personal concerns
b) attitudes
c) opinions
d) empathy
e) identification with character
f) sensitivity to ranges of feelings of the characters
g) or what?

1.5 *CHARACTERS AS REPRESENTATIVES OF CHILDHOOD*
Does the author through use of characterisation offer a vivid and direct picture of childhood experience by:
a) describing real life events
b) describing real characters
c) telling anecdotes
d) inventing characters
e) writing a fantasy
f) or how?

2.0 PLOT

2.1 *QUALITY OF PLOT*
Does the writing tell a good story?
a) is there action
b) an interesting situation
c) does it arouse our expectations
d) is there a climax
e) is the ending successful
f) or what?

2.2 *QUALITY OF CONSTRUCTION OF PLOT*
Has the author handled the plot successfully by:
a) telling a logical sequence
b) relating prior events to present occurrences
c) constructing an effective plot
d) moving forwards in time
e) moving backwards in time
f) writing in the present form
g) sustaining the plot throughout
h) testing cognitive hypotheses
i) making sense of the world
j) or how?

2.3 *ORIGIN OF PLOT*
Is there any evidence to suggest that television, literature, or a personal experience has provided a stimulus for the plot by providing adequate nourishment for:
a) imaginative play
b) cognitive development
c) affective development
d) retelling of the stimulus
e) describing experiences
f) or what?

2.4 *EVIDENCE OF PERSONAL EXPERIENCE AS PLOT*

Does the plot reflect any of the following examples of universality of experience?
a) a journey
b) a quest
c) a need for security
d) shrinking
e) growing
f) joy
g) happiness
h) disappointment
i) despair
j) or what?

3.0 SETTING

3.1 *PLACE OR SCENE*

Where does the story take place?
a) in the present
b) in the past
c) in the future
d) in the real world
e) in an imaginary world
f) or where?

3.2 *DETAILS OF SCENE*

Does the author show a sensitivity to the demands of his environment by:
a) strongly visual description
b) vividly colourful description
c) an eye for detail
d) acute perception
e) use of senses
f) or how?

3.3 *RESHAPING EXPERIENCE*

Is there any evidence to suggest that the author has reshaped the world so that he is:
a) part of the setting
b) would like to be in part of the setting
c) has enjoyed being part of the setting
d) would hate to be part of the setting
e) or what?

4.0 STYLE

4.1 *EFFECTIVENESS OF WRITING AS STORY*

Is there any evidence of the following which would indicate that the writing is an effective story?
a) appropriate beginning
b) appropriate ending
c) use of subjective narrative

d) use of 3rd person
e) adequate control of spelling
f) adequate control of punctuation
g) adequate control of structure
h) adequate control of lexical choice
i) or what?

4.2 *APPROPRIATENESS*
Is the language used by the author:
a) appropriate
b) effective
c) decorative
d) inventive
e) original
f) exaggerated
g) conventional
h) formal
i) natural
j) or what?

4.3 *STYLE OF DISCOURSE*
Is the relationship between the participants in the story:
a) colloquial
b) formal
c) casual
d) ceremonial
e) personal
f) impersonal
g) or what?

4.4 *USES OF LANGUAGE*
Does the author through characterisation use language to:
a) predict
b) imagine
c) reflect
d) project
e) reminisce
f) retell
g) report
h) or what?

4.5 *SENSORY IMAGES*
Does the author employ any of the following larger scale characteristics in order to create mood?
a) personification
b) metaphor
c) simile
d) onomatopoeia
e) repetition
f) patterning
g) denotation
h) connotation
i) or what?

References

APPLEBEE, A. N. (1982) 'Writing and Learning in School Settings', in NYSTRAND, M. (ed.) op. cit.

BAETENS BEARDSMORE, H. (1982) *Bilingualism: Basic Principles*, Multicultural Matters, Clevedon: TIETO

BAZALGETTE, C. (ed.) (1989) *Primary Media Education: A Curriculum Statement*, BFI Education Department

BEAN, M. A. (1979) 'Children's Storywriting' (B.Ed. Hons unpublished thesis)

BEAN, M. A. (1985) 'An Experiment in Advance Planning' (M.Ed. unpublished thesis)

BEARD, R. (1984) *Children's Writing in the Primary School*, Hodder & Stoughton in association with UKRA

BENNETT, N. (1976) *Teaching Styles and Pupil Progress*, Open Books

BENNETT, N. *et al.* (1980) 'Open Plan Schools: Teaching, Curriculum, Design' report of the School's Council Project 'Open Plan Schools: An Enquiry (5-11)', NFER

BEREITER, C. (1980) 'Development in Writing' in GREGG, L. and STEINBERG, E. op. cit.

BEREITER C. and SCARDAMALIA, M. (1982) 'From Conversation to Composition: the role of instruction in a development process' in GLASER, R. (ed.) *Advances in instructional psychology*, 2, Hillsdale, New Jersey: Lawrence Erlbaum

BEREITER, C. and SCARDAMALIA, M. (1985) 'Children's Difficulties in Learning to Compose' in WELLS, G. and NICHOLLS, J. *Language and Learning: an interactional perspective*, The Falmer Press

BRITTON, J. (1970) *Language and Learning*, Penguin

BRITTON, J. (1977) 'The Role of Fantasy' in MEEK, M. *et al.* op. cit.

BRITTON, J. *et al.* (1975) *The Development of Writing Abilities 11-18*, Schools Council, Macmillan Educational

BROWNJOHN, S. (1980) *Does It Have to Rhyme?* Hodder and Stoughton

BROWNJOHN, S. (1982) *What Rhymes with Secret?* Hodder and Stoughton

BRUNER, J. S. (1959) 'Learning and Thinking' *Harvard Educational Review* Vol. 29, Summer 1959, 186

BRUNER, J. S. (1962) *On Knowing: essays for the left hand*, Oxford University Press

BURGESS, A. (1977) 'Telling Stories: what the young writer does' in MEEK, M. *et. al.* op. cit.

BURTIS, P., BEREITER, C., SCARDAMALIA, M. and TETROE, J. (1983) 'The Development of Planning in Writing' in KROLL, B. and WELLS, G. *Explorations in the Development of Writing: theory, research and practice*, New York: John Wiley

CUMMINS, J. (1984) 'Bilingualism and Special Education' *Issues in Assessment and Pedagogy*, Cleveland

CUMMINS, J., and SWAIN, M. (1986) *Bilingualism in Education: aspects of theory research and practice*, Longman

DE BONO, E. (1967) *The Use of Lateral Thinking*, Jonathan Cape

DES/WO (1975) *A Language for Life* (the Bullock Report), HMSO

DES/WO (1978) *HMI Primary School's Survey*, HMSO

DES/WO (1982) *HMI First School's Survey*, HMSO

DES/WO (1985) *Education for All: the report of the* [...]
  of children from ethnic minority groups (the Swa[...]
DES/WO (1988) *English for Ages 5-11* (the Cox Rep[...]
DES/WO (1989a) *English in the National Curriculum* [...]
DES/WO (1989b) *English for Ages 5-16,* HMSO
DES/WO (1989c) *Technology for Ages 5-16,* HMSO
DES/WO (1990) *History for Ages 5-16,* HMSO
DIXON, J., STRATTA, L. (1986) 'Argument and the Teaching [...] ish: [...]
  analysis' in WILKINSON, A. (ed.) op. cit.
DOWNING, J. (1984) 'A Source of Cognitive Confusion for Beginning Readers:
  Learning in a Second Language' in *The Reading Teacher,* January
FITZPATRICK, F. (1984) *The Open Door* (The Bradford Bilingual Project) BICC
FLOWER, L. and HAYES, J. (1980a) 'The Cognition of Discovery: defining a rhetorical
  problem' *College Composition and Communication* [...] 21-33
FLOWER, L. and HAYES, J. (1980b) 'The Dynamics of Composing: making plans and
  juggling constraints' in GREGG, L. and STEINBERG, E. op. cit.
FLOWER, L. and HAYES, J. (1981) 'Plans that Guide the Composing Process' in
  FREDERIKSEN, C. and DOMINIC, J. 'The Nature, Development and Teaching of
  Written Communication', *Writing: Process, Development and Communication* Vol. 2,
  Hillsdale, New Jersey: Lawrence Erlbaum
GALTON, M. *et al.* (1980) *Inside the Primary Classroom,* Routledge & Kegan Paul
GARLAND, R. (1982) *Microcomputers and Children in the School,* Falmer Press
GREGG, L. and STEINBERG, E. (1980) *Cognitive Processes in Writing: an
  interdisciplinary approach*, Hillsdale, New Jersey: Lawrence Erlbaum
GRAVES, D. (1984) *A Researcher Learns to Write,* Heinemann Educational
GREEN, N. (ed.) (1986) *As Far as the Eye Can See,* Bradford Metropolitan Council
HARPIN, W, (1976) *The Second 'R',* Unwin Books
HARRIS, J., HORNER, S., TUNNARD, L., 'All in a Week's Work' a report on the first
  stage of the Sheffield Writing at the Transition Project, SCDC
HARRISON, B. (1983) *Learning through Writing,* NFER Nelson
HEANEY, P. (1984) 'More Like Adults' *Times Educational Supplement* 25 May
JEFFCOATE, R. (1979) *Positive Image — Towards a Multiracial Curriculum,* Chameleon
JONES, R. (1968) *Fantasy and Feeling in Education,* New York University
JONES, R. (1973) *Involving Fantasies and Feelings in Facts and Feelings in the Classroom,*
  Ward Lock Educational
JUNG, C. (1964) *Man and His Symbols,* Aldus Books
KAPPAS, K. (1967) 'A Developmental Analysis of Children Responses to Literature'
  in FENWICK, S. (ed.) *A Critical Approach to Children's Literature,* University of
  Chicago Press
KINNEAVY, J. (1971) *A Theory of Discourse,* New York: W. W. Norton
LAVENDER, R. (1977) 'Living by Fact or Fiction' *Times Educational Supplement,*
  18 November
LEECH, G. (1966) *English in Advertising,* Longman
MARTIN, N. (1971) 'What Are They Up To?' in JONES, A. and MULFORD, J. *Children
  using Language,* Oxford University Press
MARTIN, N. (1976) *Writing and Learning Across the Curriculum 11-16,* Ward Lock
  Educational
MARTLEW, M. (1983) *The Psychology of Writing Language, Development and Educational
  Perspectives,* New York: John Wiley
MEEK, M. *et al.* (1977) *The Cool Web,* Bodley Head
McLAUGHLIN, B. (1978) *Second Language Acquisition in Childhood,* Hillsdale, New
  Jersey: Lawrence Erlbaum
NCC (1989) *Non-statutory Guidance, English: Key Stage 1,* HMSO
NOBLE, P. (1985) *Curriculum Planning in Primary History* No. 51, Historical Association
NYSTRAND, M. (ed.) (1982) *What Writers Know,* New York: Academic Press
O'SHEA, T. (1984) 'Team Effort' *Times Educational Supplement,* 25 May
PAPERT, S. (1980) *Mindstorms,* Harvester Press

969) *Teaching the Reading of Fiction*, New York: Teachers' College Press

1967) *Seeing to the Heart*, Chatto & Windus

, C. and ROSEN, H. (1974) *The Language of Primary School Children*, Penguin

DAMALIA, M. BEREITER, C. and GOELMAN, A. (1982) 'The Role of Production Factors in Writing Ability' in NYSTRAND, M. (ed.) op. cit.

SCARDAMALIA, M. and BEREITER, C. (1983) 'The Development of Evaluative, Diagnostic and Remedial Capabilities in Children's Composing' in MARTLEW, M. op. cit.

SCHANK, R. and ABELSON, R. (1977) *Scripts, Plans, Goals and Understanding: an inquiry into human knowledge structure*, Hillsdale, New Jersey: Lawrence Erlbaum

SHAYER, D. (1972) *The Teaching of English in Schools, 1900-1972*, Routledge & Kegan Paul

SMITH, F. (1982) *Writing and the Writer*, Heinemann Educational

SMITH, F. (1984a) *Reading Like a Writer*, Centre for the Teaching of Reading in association with Abel Press, British Columbia

SMITH, F. (1984b) *Joining the Literacy Club*, Centre for the Teaching of Reading in association with Abel Press, British Columbia

SMITH, F. (1984c) *Learning to be a Critical Thinker*, Centre for the Teaching of Reading in association with Abel Press, British Columbia

SMITH, F. (1984d) *The Promise and Threat of Microcomputers in Language Education*, Centre for the Teaching of Reading in association with Abel Press, British Columbia

STEVENS, A. (1987) 'Change: A Constant Theme' *Journal of Education in Museums* 8, 15-17, Chas. Goater and Sons

TORRANCE, B. P. (1963) *Education and the Creative Potential*, University of Minnesota

VYGOTSKY, L. S. (1962) *Thought and Language*, Cambridge, Mass.: MIT Press

WAGSTAFF, P. E. (1987) 'Devising and Implementing Policies for Changing Attitudes to Racism in Primary Schools' (M.Ed. unpublished thesis)

WELLS, G. and NICHOLS, J. (1985) *Language and Learning: an interactional perspective*, Falmer Press

WILKINSON, A. (1978) 'Criteria for Language Development' *Educational Review*, Vol. 30, No. 1

WILKINSON, A. (ed.) (1986) *The Writing of Writing*, Open University Press

WILLIAMS, J. (1977) *Learning to Write or Writing to Learn?* NFER

WITKIN, R. (1974) *The Intelligence of Feeling*, Heinemann Education

YAMAMOTO, K. (1972) *The Child and His Image*, Boston: Houghton Mifflin